60 Home-Style Recipes that Capture the Country's

Vegan Treasures
of India

Anusha Moorthy Santosh
Creator of YummyYatra

PAGE STREET
PUBLISHING CO.

PAGE STREET
PUBLISHING CO.

First published in 2023 by
Page Street Publishing Co.
27 Congress Street, Suite 1511
Salem, MA 01970
www.pagestreetpublishing.com

Distributed by Macmillan, sales in Canada by The Canadian Manda Group.

27   26   25   24   23   1   2   3   4   5

ISBN-13: 978-1-64567-908-0
ISBN-10: 1-64567-908-X

Library of Congress Control Number: 2022947316

Cover and book design by Katie Beasley for Page Street Publishing Co.
Photography by Anusha Moorthy Santosh

Printed and bound in the United States

Dedication

To the women in my life—ammamma, Mummy and Gaia. I owe my love
and appreciation of good food and cooking to you.

To my dad, the coolest and the best.

Love you forever.

Contents

Introduction

India. It's not easy to know how and where to start. Is it even possible to capture India's essence in the introduction of a cookbook?

I recently read an article about how Indian-style pizza is becoming the next best pizza style in America, especially among non-Indians. While I was happy to see that more and more people are beginning to appreciate Indian flavors, a part of me wished to see a different kind of headline. What does "Indian-style" even mean? Curry on a pizza? I am not against fusion food of any kind, because I myself grew up eating macaroni upma, za'atar-stuffed parātha and cilantro-chutney spread over khubz. These are foods that came out of circumstances—or assimilation foods. And, of course, I agree that almost all cuisines, in a way, have some fusion element because of foreign invasions and migrations. It is impossible to put Indian cuisine in a neat little box because it draws on the myriad customs, traditions, cultures and microclimates in the vast country that India is. Dishes vary greatly by region, by city, by household. The food that people eat changes every few miles, much like the language and culture. A lot of people divide the country's cuisine into North, South, East and West, but I feel no such division can cover the entirety of Indian cooking.

At a vegan meetup a few years ago, a person relatively new to Indian culture excitedly mentioned, "I love Indian dāl. How do you guys make it?" To that, my fellow Indian Americans and I gave a variety of responses. Each one of us had a completely different name for our favorite dāl, the method of cooking it and the type of lentil used to make our home-style dāl. The person who asked us the question was quite stunned and overwhelmed with the responses. And we all ganged up (in a good way) to educate him that each one of us could provide him with at least four more dāl recipes. You get the picture—one dish, many avatars. That is Indian cuisine.

I, too, am like the Indian dāl. Many years ago, when I was living in Memphis, a person asked my husband, Santosh, and me what part of India my family was from. She was asking because there were various Indian regional associations in the city, and she wanted to know if I was interested in joining the one that represented the Indian state where our families came from. We had no specific answer, as we genuinely felt that we could belong to almost every regional association that existed at that time. My parents were born in Kerala, a southern state, but we speak Tamil because their families are not from Kerala but from Tamil Nadu, where Tamil is spoken. I was born near Jamshedpur, which is a city in yet another state in the eastern part of India, because that was my mother's hometown. My father's side of the family had relocated to Bombay (now Mumbai) in the late sixties, so his hometown was Bombay. My explanation to that person did not end there. I had to continue to tell her that I did not really grow up in India, and that visits to India from the Middle East were just an annual tradition to meet grandparents, uncles, aunts and cousins in different parts of the country. Later on, I lived in other countries for some time before moving to the United States and have lived here for quite some time.

Food has always been my family's love language. My parents always cooked with the best ingredients, and every dish made at home was made from scratch. Dishes from all over India and the Middle East were cooked in my mom's kitchen, and the conversations my brother, Chirag, and I most enjoyed revolved around food. I always found myself in the kitchen watching and learning the food, customs and traditions from my parents. Now I know I was actually soaking up all that knowledge.

The food I grew to love are the dishes I remember my mom making in her kitchen, dishes I made for the first time, dishes I made for my husband's lunch box while we lived in Singapore and Belgium, dishes my dad experimented on over the weekend and dishes I loved eating in Indian streets and restaurants. Food my family loves. My now family—my husband, our daughter, Gaia, and I—love to travel. Gaia has been a geography enthusiast since she was a fifteen-month-old kid, and her interest has only grown as she grew older. Our love for food, travel and cultures and my love for photography are the reasons behind me starting YummyYatra (yummyyatra.com or @yummyyatra).

I strongly feel that Indian cuisine outside India doesn't get its due because it is understood only through the lens of what Indian restaurants offer on their menus. Indian food gets stereotyped into its most popular dishes—palak paneer, biryani, naan or the Southern dosa—and the real essence of what Indian families eat in their homes is lost. In India, people go to restaurants to celebrate and spend time with friends, and they order food that they do not ordinarily make at home—that is the culture. So thousands of tasty, nutritious and popular dishes that people eat in their homes everyday remain underappreciated. A wealth of Indian culinary culture and traditions remain unknown. This is even more true for vegan foodies since many of these stereotypical dishes contain dairy.

My goal, through this book, is to shine a light on the home-style dishes ("ghar ka khana") that represent the vast, underappreciated majority of Indian cuisine. And to show how much variety and depth the Indian cuisines have to offer food fanatics that happen to be vegan and how simple these dishes are to re-create in your own homes.

I have always wished for vada pav, dabeli or dosa to be a global snack, a snack everybody would recognize and love, much like pizza. When I visited Naples, Italy, this past summer, I was soaking in the pizza culture of the city. I enjoyed eating the classic (and natively vegan) marinara pizza (the OG) in various Napolitan pizzerias. A simple crust, with a heavy splash of local tomato sauce, a sprinkle of oregano and a drizzle of olive oil is all there is to it. What stood out to me is its simplicity. Pizza has metamorphosed from those humble origins in Naples to the world-wide phenomenon it is today.

I am sure if people try the simple Indian dishes in this book, they too will find a place in people's lives. With this book, my hope is that my non-Indian readers will see Indian cuisine in a different light and my Indian readers will feel proud of their cuisine and culture. My goal is to enable unknown and well-known Indian recipes, especially plant-forward ones, to gain even wider appeal, and to offer happiness not just in the eating and serving of them to your loved ones, but in the cooking of these Indian dishes as well.

With love,
Anusha

How to Use This Book

The recipes in this book are easy to make and do not require special equipment. Also, the cooking techniques are simple and approachable. I have picked out dishes from all over India that are inherently vegetarian or vegan. I do not use mock meat and, therefore, these dishes are close to the original cooking method. The only substitutes that I have used are plant-based milk to replace dairy, tofu to replace paneer, and chickpea/gram flour (besan) batter to replace whisked eggs.

Language and Pronunciation

Languages are typically combined in India, so you will find most of the recipe titles and ingredients are a combination of Hindi, English and Tamil. I refer to the ingredients by their most commonly used names (meaning the local language name printed on the packaging), which will make it easier for you while shopping for them.

When you see a non-English word with a mark over the a (ā), it denotes a long "ah" sounds like in the word father.

Useful Common Techniques and Tips

Deep-Frying

A hot kadhai wok of oil needs your undivided attention. Make sure anything you drop into the oil (including the spoon or the tongs you use) is dry. You can avoid hot oil splashes (my husband's worst nightmare) by slowly lowering the food into the oil away from you. Do not overcrowd the oil.

In recipes like Everybody's Favorite Kānda Bhajiya with Special Onion Chutney (page 23) and The Iconic Vada Pav (page 19), make sure there is enough room for each bhajiya or the vada to cook evenly. Overcrowding the pan also reduces the temperature of the oil, and the food in turn becomes oily and soggy. While frying, gently move the food around the oil with a pair of tongs or a slotted spoon so it does not burn. Set a plate or baking sheet lined with a kitchen towel or paper towels near the frying station before you start the frying process. Immediately after you remove the food from the oil, place it on the plate or baking sheet to drain the excess oil.

Tadkā

Tadkā is widely used in Indian cooking. Ground or whole spices are added to hot oil, and the flavorful oil is then added to the dish. This process of adding the spices to hot oil is called blooming. Every house has their own style of tadkā they like to use, but the most important feature of the tadkā is that it is prepared fresh and poured hot. Premaking tadkā and storing it to use later defeats the whole purpose. The fat used for the tadkā depends on the type of dish being prepared and the part of India the dish is from. Using a tadkā pan or a small skillet works best. Ghee is widely used in many Indian dishes for tadkā, but I use oil or sometimes vegan butter to keep it vegan. During the tadkā process, keep in mind that the spices and aromatics are added in quick succession—ingredients that cook quickly are added last. Therefore, have your mise en place ready because you will have no time to gather ingredients once the process has started. See the masālā dabba (image to the left).

Pāpad or Pappadām

Pāpad or pappadām is a thin and crispy wafer commonly made of rice, lentils or tapioca flour that is typically served as an accompaniment with Indian meals. There are numerous regional variations. The most well-known one, served at most Indian restaurants, uses ground urad dāl (split black lentils) that are mixed with spices and salt and made into dough. They are then shaped, sun-dried and stored for consumption. When ready to use, they are fried, roasted or microwaved.

To Fry Pāpad

Heat some oil in a wok for about 5 to 7 minutes over medium. With a pair of tongs, gently drop the pāpad into the oil. The pāpad should change color, at which time you should carefully flip it, fry on the other side for a few seconds, then take it out to drain.

To Roast Pāpad

You can roast pāpad directly on the stovetop. Just hold the pāpad using a pair of tongs over the flame. Keep flipping and turning it around to avoid burning. When it is cooked all through, turn off the heat. To roast in the microwave, simply place one pāpad on a plate and microwave on high for 15 seconds. Flip and continue, if needed. It is best to make pāpad right before serving, as they lose crunch with time.

Spices

A well-seasoned dish is what takes it from ordinary to extraordinary. Layering flavors, such as spices, aromatics, acids and herbs, makes great dishes. Consider buying whole spices, such as cumin and coriander seeds, instead of ground store-bought spices. They keep the flavor longer. You can simply toast these spices for a few minutes, then grind them at home in a small coffee or spice grinder, which is quite inexpensive. See garam masālā (page 165), chāt masālā (page 165) and sandwich masālā (page 17).

Cooking Oils

When you come across "neutral oil" in a recipe, you can use any oil, such as avocado oil, grape-seed oil, vegetable oil, etc., that doesn't impart strong flavor to the dish.

Other oils mentioned in this book are mustard oil, coconut oil, gingelly oil and peanut oil. Mustard oil, gingelly oil and peanut oil are available in most South Asian stores.

Chilies

Chilies are used in many recipes in this book—fresh, dried and ground. When a recipe calls for "green chili peppers," I typically use Thai or serrano peppers for Indian dishes. Feel free to use any fresh variety that you can source, and adjust the spice level according to your taste.

In recipes that call for "red chili powder," I use ground red chili pepper. I source mine from the Indian grocery store or online. If that is not accessible to you, you can use ground cayenne pepper instead.

"Kashmiri red chili powder" is a specific variety, characterized by its ability to give bright red color and flavor to food without it becoming too spicy or pungent. It lends a smoky earthiness to dishes. You can find Kashmiri chili powder at any South Asian grocery store or online.

In recipes that call for "whole dried red chilis," these are whole red chilis that have been sun-dried. It can be overwhelming when you go shopping for whole dried red chilis at any South Asian grocery store because of the huge variety. You can buy any dry variety that says "whole chilies." The spice level differs, but I recommend starting with a small quantity, tasting and adding more.

A Few Pointers to Make Your Dish Stand Out

- Taste your food during cooking. It is a good idea to taste your food at the beginning, middle and end of cooking. It will help you understand the nature of every ingredient and how each of them changes with time, heat and when mixed with other ingredients. Like the great chef Massimo Bottura says, "Follow your palate!" Then you can adjust accordingly. With Indian food, especially gravies, you can usually recover any mishaps: For example, if you add too much salt, you can dilute it with water or add a can of chickpeas or boiled potatoes. If you add too much chili, you can add some coconut milk or tomatoes.

- Cook the onions and tomatoes well. In many recipes, especially gravies, you sauté the onions, then add the tomatoes, aromatics and a few spices, sometimes water, all in quick succession. Take some time to simmer the spice-based sauce to lock in all the flavors.

- Use freshly ground spices whenever possible. It is worth buying them whole and grinding them yourself. You can find whole spices in online specialty stores or South Asian grocery stores. Some spices that I like to grind and store are the spices that I use regularly, like garam masālā (page 165), chāt masālā (page 165), whole coriander, cumin and cardamom. Of course, store-bought ground spices are fine, but make sure they are fairly fresh. When freshly ground, the spices last longer, making your food taste way better. Invest in a good-quality mortar and pestle or an electric spice grinder. They are inexpensive and worth the investment.

Delicious Dishes for Sharing and Entertaining

The dishes in this chapter are meant to bring people together. Indians love to snack. Whether on plane or train journeys, road trips, during homework time or a game day watch party, snacking happens often. But by far the best is while catching up with a friend, sharing a delicious street-food delicacy. Sharing food is one of life's great pleasures. The emotions that come from it are universal. There are so many street foods in India, and they always make the perfect snacks for sharing and entertaining when re-created at home. These street-foods and nibblers are perfect for picnics, potlucks, game days or backyard gatherings. Pretty much any kind of get-together you can imagine!

The Classic Bombay Sandwich

Grilled sandwich with a delicious green chutney, layered with vegetables and a special spice blend

A good sandwich is one that is well layered, holds together perfectly and remains crispy until the last bite. A Bombay sandwich fits all of the above, but the key is to use the right kind of bread. As soon as you take your first bite, you will soon realize that a Bombay sandwich is unlike any sandwich you've ever had. It is an explosion of flavors and textures. This simple creation is one of Mumbai's (formerly Bombay) popular street staples, and small street-side shops selling these sandwiches can be found in almost every corner in Mumbai, with everyone from college-age kids and working professionals to everyday people queuing up for a quick bite. Sandwich vallahs (sandwich vendors) strategically layer the vegetables with chutney and spices that make the assembly look like a work of art. This sandwich has a range of textures from the various vegetables that are thinly sliced, making them easy to bite through. The chutney is the perfect condiment, and the ground masālā (spice blend) is the ideal seasoning. It is easily adaptable, so feel free to adjust the filling-to-bread ratio and use more or less of any vegetable to suit your taste. The spicy chutney is essential. It perks up every bite.

Yield: 6 to 8 servings ✳ Prep Time: 15 to 20 minutes ✳ Cook Time: 7 to 8 minutes per sandwich

For the Chutney

2 bunches fresh cilantro, thoroughly washed and tough stems discarded

4 green chili peppers, or according to taste

3 cloves garlic, peeled

1 tbsp (7 g) roasted chana dāl (dalia or roasted split chickpeas)

Salt, to taste

3 ice cubes

For the Sandwich Masālā

2 tbsp (12 g) cumin seeds (jeera)

2 whole cloves (lavang)

1 tsp black peppercorns (kāli mirch)

1 tbsp (6 g) fennel seeds (saunf)

1 tbsp (8 g) āmchur powder (dry mango powder)

½ tsp ground ginger

½ tsp hing (asafoetida)

1 tbsp (12 g) kāla namak (black salt)

Salt, to taste

To make the chutney, add the cilantro to a blender along with the green chili peppers, garlic, chana dāl, salt and ice cubes. Blend to a smooth paste. Add very little water to thin it out, if needed. Store the chutney in an airtight container in the refrigerator until ready to use.

To make the sandwich masālā, heat a small skillet over medium heat, add the cumin seeds, whole cloves, black peppercorns and fennel seeds, and dry roast, stirring continuously, until fragrant, about 2 minutes. Turn off the heat. Add the āmchur powder, ground ginger, hing, kāla namak and salt. Add the mixture to a spice grinder, and grind to a fine powder.

(continued)

The Classic Bombay Sandwich (*continued*)

For Assembling

1 loaf sliced white or sourdough bread

Spreadable vegan butter, as needed

2 large bell peppers (any color), thinly sliced

2 medium onions, thinly sliced

1 large cucumber, peeled and thinly sliced

3 medium firm tomatoes, thinly sliced

1 medium beet, peeled, thinly sliced and boiled or steamed (see Tips)

2 large potatoes, thinly sliced and boiled or steamed (see Tips)

Shredded vegan mozzarella cheese, as needed, optional

For Serving

Thin sev, optional (see Tips)

More chutney or ketchup

To assemble the sandwich, place 3 slices of bread on a large cutting board. Spread vegan butter on all 3 slices, followed by a layer of the chutney. On one of the slices, layer the bell peppers, onions and cucumber, and sprinkle some sandwich masālā evenly on top of each layer of vegetable.

Place another slice of bread on top of the vegetables, chutney side up. Now, continue layering the remaining vegetables—tomatoes, beet and potatoes—while sprinkling sandwich masālā over each layer. Sprinkle with vegan mozzarella, if using.

Cover with the third slice of bread, chutney side down.

In the same skillet you use to toast the spices, heat over low heat, and brush some vegan butter. Place the sandwich in the skillet, cook on both sides until you see a crispy, brown exterior. These sandwiches can be made in an electric panini/sandwich press as well. I make them using a "jaffle iron," just like the many sandwich vallahs of Mumbai.

How to Enjoy

- Cut each sandwich into quarters, and serve them hot or at room temperature with some ketchup or green chutney. If you are making a large quantity ahead and storing them for sharing later, let the sandwiches cool completely before covering them loosely with a piece of wax paper. This will keep them from getting soggy.

- After grilling/toasting the sandwich, spread some extra chutney on top, and sprinkle some sev over the chutney. Do this just before serving.

Tips

- *Homemade sandwich masālā tastes best. Freshly made masālā can be stored in an airtight container for about a month. However, if you will not be making the sandwich masālā at home, you can find it in a well-stocked South Asian store. If you don't have access to sandwich masālā, use chāt masālā (page 165 or store-bought) instead.*

- *Thinly slice the potatoes and beet (a mandoline is recommended for this), and then microwave them (separately) in a microwave-safe bowl to cook them fast. Once cooked through, drain the water and set aside to cool for a few minutes before using the vegetables in the sandwich. They should be cooked through but still hold their shape.*

- *Sev can be found in most South Asian grocery stores or in the international aisle of well-stocked markets.*

The Iconic Vada Pav

Everyone's favorite—India's very own burger

Mumbai holds a very special place in my life. Vada pav is a part of the beating heart of this bustling city. First, a spicy, garlicky mashed potato mixture is coated in a thick chickpea flour batter and then deep-fried to golden perfection—that's your vada, or batata vada. This vada is then stuffed inside a fluffy, slider-esque bun—that's your pav. That's it! It's quite simple to understand the general idea of vada pav, yet it is so much more. The various chutneys make it an extra-special sandwich. Found in almost every corner of the city, vada pav is an emotion. It is a perfect ode to the city's hustle and on-the-go culture. If you have had a good vada pav, you know what I am talking about. If not, try this recipe. Nigella Lawson, during one of her visits to Mumbai, said about vada pav, "Best thing I have eaten in 2017."

Yield: about 15 vadas ✱ *Prep Time: 25 minutes* ✱ *Cook Time: 45 minutes*

For the Batata Vada

2 tbsp (30 ml) neutral oil, plus more for frying (see Tips)

¼ tsp black mustard seeds (rāi)

1 tsp fresh ginger, grated

4 green chili peppers, or according to taste

11 cloves garlic, peeled and crushed or minced

½ tsp ground turmeric (haldi powder)

8 potatoes (1.9 lb [865 g]), boiled, peeled and mashed

1 tbsp (15 ml) fresh lemon juice

4 cups (360 g) besan (chickpea/gram flour), sifted

Salt, to taste

To make the batata vada, in a large skillet over medium heat, heat 2 tablespoons (30 ml) of the oil until shimmering. Add the mustard seeds. When the mustard seeds begin to pop, add the ginger, green chili peppers, garlic and ground turmeric, and stir until the garlic is fragrant and light brown, about 30 seconds.

Add the mashed potatoes. Turn off the heat, and stir in the lemon juice. Mix well, then taste and adjust the seasoning, as needed. When the mixture is cool enough to handle, form it into approximately 4-inch (10-cm) diameter balls weighing about 2 ounces (57 g), and set them aside.

In a large mixing bowl, combine the besan, salt and enough water to make a smooth batter. Whisk the batter well for at least 3 minutes to incorporate air into it. This ensures a crisp and light exterior for the vada. Set the batter aside.

Pour oil in a large wok, and heat over medium heat for 3 to 4 minutes. When you drop a drop of the batter in the oil, it should instantly sizzle and float to the top. Or, if using a thermometer, the oil should register 350°F (176°C).

Meanwhile, move the batter and the potato mixture closer to the frying station. Line a cooling rack or plate with a kitchen towel.

Gently dip each potato ball into the besan batter, turning it around to coat the ball entirely. Working in batches, drop the balls into the oil carefully, and fry for about 5 minutes, turning each vada halfway through so that the batter gets cooked evenly and the vadas appear golden brown. You may need to adjust the heat to maintain the temperature of the oil. You can fry three to four vadas at a time, depending on the size of your kadhai/wok. Transfer the vadas to the kitchen towel. If you notice any bits of batter floating in oil, scoop them out onto the kitchen towel as well.

(continued)

For the Dry Chutney

2 cups (200 g) chura (fried chickpea batter bits)

12 cloves garlic, unpeeled and pierced all over with a toothpick or paring knife

½ cup (73 g) roasted, unsalted peanuts

1 tsp cumin seeds (jeera)

1 tbsp (11 g) Kashmiri red chili powder, or according to taste

Salt, to taste

For Serving

Fried green chili peppers

Fresh mint-cilantro chutney (page 164)

Dinner rolls or small slider buns

Once all the vadas are fried, dip a spoon or your fingers into the remaining besan batter, and drop the batter directly into the oil to create more bits. This is called chura, which we will use for the dry chutney. Once these batter bits appear golden, 1 to 2 minutes, remove them and drain on the kitchen towel.

Into the same oil, gently drop the pierced garlic, and fry for 30 seconds. Remove and drain the garlic on a plate.

To make the dry chutney, in a spice grinder, mix together the chura, the fried garlic, the roasted peanuts and cumin seeds, and process to a coarse mixture. Add the Kashmiri red chili powder and salt. Transfer the dry chutney to a serving bowl.

Cut a small slit in the green chili peppers, and fry them for about 10 seconds in the hot oil. Transfer them to a plate, and sprinkle them with some salt.

To assemble, slit open a bun, spoon some mint-cilantro chutney and the dry chutney, and insert the vada. Close the pav, and serve with the fried chili peppers.

How to Enjoy

The vadas are usually served hot, as soon as they are fried, in street-side shops. However, when serving a batch for a potluck or gathering, you can make the vadas in advance and cover them lightly. Assemble them in the pav with the chutneys just before eating. If carrying them for a picnic, let them cool completely, and pack the chutneys and fried chili peppers separately in airtight containers.

Tips

- *The amount of oil for frying depends on the size of the wok you use. Add enough so that when you drop the vada in the oil, they are reasonably covered in it.*
- *Store any leftover dry chutney and mint-cilantro chutney in an airtight continer in the refrigerator for up to 2 days.*

Everybody's Favorite Kanda Bhajiya with Special Onion Chutney

Classic crispy onion fritters

Kānda means "onion" in Marathi, and bhajiya means "fritters." They are also called pakodas. My ammamma (maternal grandmother) made the best bhajiyas, and always amazed her unexpected guests as she would make these perfectly crispy, addictive, piping-hot, bite-sized pieces in just a few minutes. Bhajiyas/pakodas should be eaten hot, with steam visibly coming out of them at the first bite, but they taste delicious when served at room temperature, too. Somehow, they always taste extra delicious on a rainy day. This version of onion fritters with the special spicy onion chutney is popular in Pune, a city in the western state of Maharashtra. Onions with more onions, you ask? Oh yes! Trust me. It works beautifully!

Yield: 3 to 4 servings ✳ *Prep Time: 20 minutes* ✳ *Cook Time: 45 minutes*

For the Bhajiyas

3 to 4 medium red onions, thinly sliced lengthwise, about ⅛ inch (3 mm) in width

Salt, to taste

1 tsp red chili powder or cayenne pepper, or according to taste

1 cup (92 g) besan (chickpea/gram flour)

Roughly chopped fresh cilantro, optional

1 tbsp (5 g) coriander seeds (dhaniya), gently crushed, optional

Neutral oil, for deep-frying

For the Onion Chutney

1 large red onion, finely chopped

8 tbsp (120 ml) hot frying oil from the bhajiyas

1 tsp Kashmiri red chili powder, or according to taste

½ tsp salt, or to taste

How to Enjoy

• Serve the bhajiyas hot with onion chutney, mint-cilantro chutney (page 164) or ketchup. They pair well with a cup of Invigorating Masālā Chāi (page 143).

• Bhajiyas are best eaten fresh; they lose some of their crispiness when stored.

To make the bhajiyas, in a large mixing bowl, add the sliced red onions, salt and red chili powder. Mix thoroughly, and set the bowl aside for at least 5 to 7 minutes so the onions start releasing water; this will help bind the mixture without adding extra water. A wet batter will not give you the classic crispy bhajiya/pakoda texture.

After the onions have rested, sprinkle the besan over with a spoon, a little at a time. Mix in the cilantro and coriander seeds, if using. Toss the onions, besan and spices using your hands. The dry batter will convert into a semi-wet mixture. Add just a few drops of water, if needed, to create a coating around the onions.

Prepare a plate or a wire rack next to the stovetop. Heat 2 inches (5 cm) of the oil in a deep wok over medium heat. To check if the oil is hot enough, drop a small piece of onion from the batter into the oil, and it should quickly float to the top.

Gently drop five to six 2-tablespoon (3- to 4-g) portions of the battered onions into the hot oil. Cook, turning occasionally using a slotted spoon, until the bhajiyas are golden brown all around, 3 to 4 minutes. Gently remove the bhajiyas from the oil, and transfer them to the plate to drain any excess oil. Repeat with the remaining batter.

To make the onion chutney, in a large bowl, combine the chopped red onion, oil, Kashmiri red chili powder and salt.

Tips

• *Once the batter is ready, don't delay the frying process as the onions will keep releasing water and the bhajiyas will not be crispy.*

• *Don't overcrowd the wok while frying the bhajiyas and don't move them around in the pan immediately. Wait for at least a minute, so they form a shape.*

Crunchy Makhāna Namkeen

Spiced, toasted fox nuts, a popcorn-like snack

Makhāna are dried water lily seeds, also known as fox nuts. The hardworking farmers gather the seeds by hand and clean them in water, after which the seeds are sun-dried. After this process, the seeds are quickly whacked over a high flame so that the black shells break and pop, and white puffs emerge. Fox nuts have a very similar flavor profile and texture of popcorn. They are used in savory Indian gravies, sweet dishes like kheer and as a snack when toasted and seasoned with spices, like this makhāna namkeen.

Yield: 5 servings ✳ *Prep Time: 5 minutes* ✳ *Cook Time: 25 minutes*

2 tbsp (30 ml) neutral oil, divided

6 cups (190 g) whole makhāna (fox nuts)

¼ cup (35 g) unsalted almonds

¼ cup (35 g) unsalted cashews

½ cup (100 g) roasted chana dāl (dalia or roasted split chickpeas)

10 to 12 fresh curry leaves (kadi patta), optional

¾ tsp salt, or to taste

1 tsp red chili powder or cayenne pepper, or according to taste

1 tsp kāla namak (black salt)

2 tsp (4 g) chāt masālā (homemade [see page 165] or store-bought)

In a skillet over medium heat, heat 1 tablespoon (15 ml) of the oil. Add the makhāna to the pan, and toast until they are crispy, stirring continuously, 5 to 7 minutes. Transfer the toasted makhāna to a large bowl, and set it aside to cool.

Heat the remaining tablespoon (15 ml) of oil in the skillet over medium-low heat, and add the almonds, cashews and roasted chana dāl. Continue stirring to avoid burning, about 5 minutes. Turn off the heat. Transfer the toasted nuts into the large bowl with the toasted makhāna.

To the same skillet, immediately add the curry leaves, if using. The curry leaves will wilt in the residual heat of the skillet. Once the curry leaves have wilted, add them to the toasted makhāna and nuts.

Stir in the salt, red chili powder, kāla namak and chāt masālā with the makhāna and nuts, and toss well so that the spices coat the nuts and the makhāna evenly.

How to Enjoy

Serve the makhāna namkeen at room temperature. If storing for later use, make sure to put the makhāna namkeen in an airtight container, and they will keep fresh for about 2 weeks at room temperature. They may lose their crunch, in which case you can sauté them in a skillet for about 2 minutes.

Spongy Ravā Dhokla

Soft, spongy steamed savory cake-bites

When you need an impressive and super easy appetizer for sharing with friends, make this quick ravā dhokla. Dhokla is a steamed snack made with a savory batter along with chili peppers, ginger and a spicy, aromatic tadkā. There are many infinite variations, gosh; it is hard to pick a favorite kind. But when I have to get something on the table quickly for a group of friends, I always make this version. I had one in Ahmedabad years ago; the flavors, texture and aroma were simply magical.

Yield: 4 servings ✳ *Prep Time: 15 minutes* ✳ *Cook Time: 25 minutes*

For the Batter

1 cup (170 g) fine ravā or sooji (semolina) (see Tips)

1 tsp fresh ginger, grated

1 green chili pepper, or according to taste, finely chopped

1 tsp neutral oil, plus more for greasing the pan

¼ tsp granulated sugar

1½ tbsp (21 ml) lemon juice

Salt, to taste

½ cup (120 ml) water

1 tsp Eno® fruit salt, or substitute ¾ tsp baking soda (see Tips)

For Tadkā (Tempering)

1 tbsp (15 ml) neutral oil

½ tsp black mustard seeds (rāi)

1 tsp white sesame seeds (til)

Pinch of hing (asafoetida)

6 to 8 curry leaves (kadi patta), optional

For Serving

Chopped fresh cilantro

How to Enjoy

• Serve the cut pieces of dhokla warm or at room temperature with mint-cilantro chutney (page 164).

• For a picnic, pack the dhokla and the cilantro separately. Sprinkle the cilantro over the dholka just before serving.

In a large mixing bowl, mix together the ravā, ginger, green chili, oil, sugar, lemon juice, salt and water. Set the batter aside to rest for a few minutes.

Meanwhile, prepare a large Dutch oven with a small steel trivet set inside, and pour in about 2 cups (240 ml) of water. Bring the water to a boil. Grease a cake pan that will fit into the Dutch oven with oil.

Add the Eno® fruit salt to the batter in the mixing bowl, mix the batter, and quickly pour it into the prepared cake pan. Spread the batter evenly by shaking the pan a few times. Place the cake pan on top of the trivet in the Dutch oven. Cover the Dutch oven with a lid, and steam the batter over medim heat until a toothpick inserted comes out clean, 15 to 20 minutes.

Remove the cake pan, and allow it to cool for a few minutes while you prepare the tadkā (tempering).

For the tadkā, heat a small skillet over medium heat. Add the oil, and allow it to warm. Add the black mustard seeds. After they begin to pop, gently add the white sesame seeds, hing and the curry leaves, if using. Turn off the heat, and carefully add 3 tablespoons (45 ml) of water to the tempering. Pour the tempering mixture over the steamed dhokla.

Top the dhokla with fresh cilantro, and slice them into squares or diamonds.

Tips

• *Look for fine semolina in any South Asian store. The names on the pack may be semolina, ravā, sooji/suji and cream of wheat. You can use any kind of steamer pot or the steam setting of an Instant Pot to cook the dhokla. Just make sure you use a cake pan or vessel that easily fits into the steamer pot that you will be using.*

• *Eno® fruit salt is available in most South Asian grocery stores in small bottles or sachets. If you cannot find it, use baking soda instead.*

Delightful Sev Puri

Crispy crackers topped with crunchy toppings and tongue-tickling condiments

Chāt—In India, chāt is a way of life. It describes an entire category of Indian street food or set of snacks that can be enjoyed anytime. It offers a combination of crispy, crunchy, spicy, tangy and sweet components. There are hundreds of chāt varieties, but if I had to choose my favorite, it would be sev puri. While it is best enjoyed in the streets of India, engaging all five senses, I do enjoy making it at home because it comes pretty close to the original with the use of freshly made chutneys. The sum of this dish is greater than its parts, but the parts are wonderful, too. Each part plays an important role here: the seasoned potatoes; tangy, sweet and spicy chutneys; fresh vegetables; the chāt masāla; the crunchy sev and the crisp puris. Sev puri is perfect for entertaining. The different components can be made ahead, the assembly is easy, and they look beautiful no matter how you serve them, whether on a board or on individual plates.

*Yield: 4 servings * Prep Time: 20 minutes * Cook Time: 1 hour (including making chutneys)*

14 puris or papdi (flat crisps) (see Tips)

1 large potato, boiled, salted, mashed and cooled

1 medium onion, finely chopped

1 medium firm tomato, finely chopped

Chāt masāla, a pinch per puri, or to taste (homemade [see page 165] or store-bought)

Mint-cilantro chutney, ¼ tsp per puri, or to taste (page 164)

A tiny drop of garlic chutney per puri, or to taste (page 164)

1 tsp date-tamarind chutney per puri, or to taste (page 164)

1 tsp nylon or fine sev per puri, or to taste (see Tips)

Fresh cilantro, finely chopped

Handful of pomegranate arils, optional

2 tbsp (15 g) raw green mango, peeled and finely chopped, optional

Handful of masāla chana dāl, optional (see Tips)

Before you begin to assemble, make sure you have all the components ready.

Place all the puris on a plate or serving board, and top each one with a bit of the potatoes. Top the potatoes with some chopped onion, then with some chopped tomato. Sprinkle chāt masāla on each puri.

Now add the three different chutneys on each puri.

Sprinkle sev on each puri, followed by cilantro, pomegranate arils, raw mango and masāla chana dāl, if using.

Serve immediately. You can make another serving if and when needed.

How to Enjoy

Serve the freshly assembled sev puri on small individuals plates or a large board.

Tips

- *You can add more or less of any component to suit your taste. I like to add more of the sweet and the spicy chutney and just a drop of the garlic chutney on each one. You can make a few and see what flavors you like the most, and then add accordingly.*

- *Puris and sev are sold in packs at most South Asian stores.*

- *Spiced masāla chana dāl is sold in packs by various brands such as Haldiram's, Mirch Masāla, etc.*

- *If you have the three types of chutney and potatoes ready in advance, you can assemble the puris in just a few minutes.*

Masaledar Tofu Tikka

Spiced and marinated grilled tofu

Here is a plant-based spin on the popular paneer tikkā. Tikkā refers to skewered food that has been marinated then barbecued or tandoori baked. The tofu acts as a perfect base for all the wonderful flavors from the warm spices. Grilling is a great option for tofu because it adds smokiness and makes it extra satisfying.

Yield: 4 servings ✳ *Prep Time: 10 minutes* ✳ *Cook Time: 45 minutes (plus marinating time)*

2 tsp (3 g) cumin seeds (jeera)

2 tsp (4 g) fennel seeds (saunf)

⅔ cup (160 ml) neutral oil, plus more for brushing

Salt, to taste

2 tsp (3 g) red chili powder or cayenne pepper (lāl mirch powder), or according to taste

2 tsp (4 g) garam masālā (homemade [see page 165] or store-bought)

½ tsp ground turmeric (haldi powder)

1 tbsp (6 g) ground coriander (dhaniya powder)

3 cloves garlic, minced

1 tbsp (6 g) fresh ginger, grated

1 cup (240 ml) unsweetened dairy-free plain yogurt, whisked

1 (16-oz [454-g]) pack extra-firm or super-firm tofu, drained, pressed and cut into blocks

Mint-cilantro chutney, for serving (page 164)

Chāt masālā (homemade [see page 165] or store-bought), for serving

Fresh lemon wedges, for serving

How to Enjoy

Serve the tofu skewers on a platter with mint-cilantro chutney (page 164) drizzled on top, a sprinkle of chāt masālā and some lemon wedges on the side.

In a small skillet on medium heat, toast the cumin seeds and fennel seeds for 2 minutes or until fragrant. Transfer the seeds to a spice grinder or a mortar and pestle. Let the seeds cool, and then finely grind to a powder.

In a large mixing bowl, combine the oil, the freshly ground cumin and fennel, the salt, red chili powder, garam masālā, ground turmeric, ground coriander, garlic, ginger and yogurt. Mix well to combine.

Gently add the tofu to the mixing bowl, and toss to coat. You may add a few drops of water if the marinade appears too thick. Let the tofu rest in the marinade in the refrigerator for at least an hour or up to 8 hours.

Heat a grill pan on medium.

Remove the tofu from the bowl, and thread them onto skewers (see Tips), about 3 to 4 per skewer, and brush the tofu with oil. Brush the grill pan with oil as well. Grill the tofu on the pan until grill marks appear and the marinade appears less drippy, about 15 minutes. Make sure you turn the skewers halfway through to ensure even cooking. You can also cook the tofu on the grill pan for 5 minutes to set the marinade on the surface of the tofu, and then cook them directly on an open flame until they appear charred.

Tips

- *This recipe can easily be doubled. You can add fresh vegetables such onions and bell peppers to the skewers. Just marinade them with the tofu. You may need to adjust the quantity of the yogurt and the spices.*

- *If you're using wood skewers, be sure to soak them in water for at least 20 minutes before skewering the tofu. This will prevent the ends of the skewers from catching fire.*

- *Be careful while handling the tofu as it tends to break easily after sitting in the marinade for some time.*

- *If the tofu sticks to the pan, use any metal spatula to gently release it. Reduce the heat slightly and continue to cook.*

Refreshing Masala Lemon Shikanji

Lemonade with a spicy kick

Here is a spiced version of the simple nimbu pani, a staple of summer in India. The popular street version is sold in places called juice centers in India. This sweet, salty, tangy drink is one you can make effortlessly and present elegantly to your guests.

Yield: 2 servings ✳ Prep Time: 5 minutes ✳ Cook Time: 10 minutes

Juice of 3 lemons or limes

2 tbsp (15 g) confectioners' sugar (see Tips)

1 tsp ground black pepper (kāli mirch)

2 tsp (12 g) ground coriander (dhaniya powder)

½ tsp kāla namak (black salt)

1 tsp ground cumin (jeera powder) (see Tips)

5 to 7 fresh mint leaves, plus a couple more per glass, for serving

Ice-cold water or ice-cold seltzer water (see Tips)

1 lemon or lime, sliced, for serving

In two tall serving glasses, combine the lemon or lime juice, sugar, ground black pepper, ground coriander, kāla namak and ground cumin.

Using a muddler or a mortar and pestle, lightly crush the mint leaves, and equally distribute them between the two glasses.

Top the glasses with chilled water.

How to Enjoy

Serve chilled with lemon slices and a few fresh mint leaves. You can also make a big batch in a pitcher and chill until it is time to serve. If you use seltzer or club soda, add it just before serving.

Tips

- *Sugar is needed to balance the tart and salty flavors. You may add it according to your preference. You can use any variety of sweeteners.*
- *Freshly toasted and ground cumin makes this drink taste even better. Heat a skillet, add a teaspoon of cumin seeds, toast them for a minute, let them cool and then grind using a spice grinder.*
- *Plain water, seltzer water or club soda all work well.*

Delectable Dal Pakwan

Crispy, deep-fried puris dunked in creamy dāl and chutneys

Dāl pakwan is synonymous with the Sindhi cuisine, which is little known, even among those from South Asia. I had first heard of dāl pakwan from our Sindhi neighbor years ago. I never tasted it until I visited Jodhpur in Rajasthan several years later. The aroma of frying pakwans and jalebis attracted me to the small street-side shop. My husband and I shared a small plate of dāl pakwan, and then I went down a dāl pakwan rabbit hole. It is essentially dāl and spiced lentils, served with pakwan, crispy puris that are flat discs made of flour. There are so many variations of this dish, including the way the dāl is simmered and the kind of dāl used; sometimes it is just one dāl, at other times a combination of three. The spices also vary. I have visited several areas in Mumbai with a huge Sindhi population and have tried different varieties of the dish during my visits. This is a re-creation that everyone in my family loves.

Yield: 4 servings or about 8 pakwans ✳ *Prep Time: 25 minutes* ✳ *Cook Time: 1 hour (plus soaking and dough resting time)*

For the Dāl

1½ cups (300 g) chana dāl (dalia or roasted split chickpeas), rinsed and soaked in 2 cups (480 ml) of warm water for at least 30 minutes

Salt, to taste

1 tsp ground turmeric (haldi powder)

1 green chili pepper, split lengthwise, or according to taste

1 tbsp (6 g) ground coriander (dhaniya powder)

½ tsp ground cumin (jeera powder)

¼ tsp red chili powder (lāl mirch) or cayenne pepper

1 tsp āmchur powder (dry mango powder)

1 tbsp (15 ml) neutral oil

1 tbsp (6 g) cumin seeds (jeera)

Pinch of hing (asafoetida)

In a pressure cooker, combine the chana dāl, salt, ground turmeric and green chili pepper with about 2½ cups (600 ml) of water. Cook on low for about 7 minutes, then allow the pressure to release naturally. Stir in the ground coriander, ground cumin, red chili powder and āmchur powder.

If you do not have a pressure cooker, put the dāl in a heavy-bottomed pot with approximately 5 cups (1.2 liters) water, and bring to a boil. Remove any scum with a spoon and discard. Add the salt, ground turmeric and green chili pepper, and cover. Reduce the heat, and simmer gently until the dāl is tender, 45 to 60 minutes, stirring every 15 minutes.

Meanwhile, for the pakwan, in a large bowl, combine the flour, cumin seeds, carom seeds, salt and 1 tablespoon (15 ml) of the oil. Mix well, and gradually add about ½ cup (120 ml) water. You may need a few more spoonfuls of water depending on the variety of flour (see Tips). Knead until you get a smooth dough with a stiff consistency, 7 to 8 minutes. Rub the remaining tablespoon (15 ml) of oil over the surface of the dough.

Cover the dough with a damp kitchen towel, and set it aside to rest for a few minutes while you prepare the tadkā for the dāl.

For the tadkā, heat 1 tablespoon (15 ml) of oil in a small skillet until shimmering, then add the cumin seeds and a pinch of hing. Once the cumin seeds begin to sizzle, turn off the heat, and pour the tadkā over the dāl. Immediately cover the dāl until ready to serve to retain the flavors.

(continued)

For the Pakwan

2 cups (250 g) all-purpose flour, sifted

1 tsp cumin seeds (jeera)

1 tsp carom seeds (ajwain)

Salt, to taste

2 tbsp (30 ml) neutral oil, divided, plus more for frying

For Serving

1 large red onion, thinly sliced

1 large boiled potato, cut into cubes, seasoned with salt, red chili powder and ground coriander

Lemon wedges

Pomegranate arils, optional

Sev, optional (see Tips)

Date-tamarind chutney (page 164)

Mint-cilantro chutney (page 164)

To fry the pakwan, preheat 3 inches (7.6 cm) of oil in a 5- to 6-inch- (13- to 15-cm-) deep skillet over medium heat. Meanwhile, knead the dough once again for 30 seconds, and divide into small balls.

Using a rolling pin, flatten, and roll out each ball, approximately 8 to 10 inches (20 to 25 cm) in diameter. Prick the flattened dough using a fork. Cover the flattened dough and any remaining dough balls.

Gently drop a small piece of dough into the hot oil to check if it is ready for frying. If it is, the dough should immediately sizzle upon contact with the hot oil and float to the surface.

Gently drop the pricked dough into the oil, reduce the heat to medium-low, and fry on both sides until crisp and golden, about 2 minutes per side. Repeat with the remaining pricked and rolled out dough.

How to Enjoy

- Serve the crispy pakwan with hot dāl and the red onion, potato, lemon wedges, pomegranate arils, sev and/or chutneys, if desired.

- The dāl can be stored in the refrigerator for later use. Reheat in a saucepan on the stovetop, and add a few spoonfuls of hot water to thin it out, if needed. The pakwan may be stored in an airtight container; however, they lose their crispy texture over time.

Tips

- *You can find different types of sev in any South Asian store. Use any variety.*
- *You may need to add more water to knead the dough to get a soft, un-sticky, dough. If the dough appears too sticky, sprinkle some flour onto the dough. If there is still dry flour remaining in the mixing bowl, add water, a few drops at a time to incorporate everything.*

Appetizing Aloo Tikki-Chole

Crispy potato patty with chickpea stew

A street-food favorite in so many cities, aloo tikki-chole is a crispy potato patty or croquette called aloo tikki, served with chole, a spiced chickpea stew. The various flavors and textures make this a popular chāt. I could eat aloo tikki endlessly without getting bored (or embarrassed). When I am able to plan in advance, I use dry chickpeas to make the chole, but I like to use canned chickpeas when I have a sudden craving for it or when I have unexpected guests.

Yield: 4 to 6 servings ✳ *Prep Time: 10 minutes* ✳ *Cook Time: 90 minutes*

For the Aloo Tikki

8 to 10 medium potatoes, boiled (see Tips)

Salt, to taste

2 tbsp (12 g) ground coriander (dhaniya powder)

1 tbsp (6 g) ground cumin (jeera powder)

2 tsp (5 g) āmchur powder (dry mango powder)

Finely chopped fresh cilantro, to taste, plus more for serving

⅓ cup (40 g) cornstarch

Neutral oil, for shallow frying

For the aloo tikki, mash the potatoes, and cool them completely. Add salt, ground coriander, ground cumin, āmchur powder, cilantro and cornstarch, and mix until well combined. Check seasoning and adjust according to taste.

Take a big spoonful (about 2 ounces [57 g]) of the potato mixture, shape it into a ball, and gently flatten it to make a tikki (patty). Repeat with the remaining potato mixture.

Heat a nonstick skillet over medium-low heat, and add a few spoons of oil. Gently place the tikki in the skillet, reduce the heat to low, and cook until it turns crisp and golden, 3 to 4 minutes.

Flip the tikki gently using a flat turner, and cook on the other side. You can shallow-fry three to four tikkis at a time, depending on the size of your pan. Turn off the heat, and place the tikkis on a plate.

(continued)

For the Chole

1 tbsp (15 ml) neutral oil

1 tbsp (6 g) cumin seeds (jeera)

1 large onion, finely chopped, plus more for serving

Salt, to taste

1 tbsp (6 g) ground coriander (dhaniya powder)

1 tsp chili powder or cayenne pepper

1 tbsp (6 g) fresh ginger, grated, plus extra fresh ginger, julienned, for serving

1 tbsp (16 g) tomato paste

1½ tbsp (9 g) garam masālā (homemade [page 165] or store-bought)

4 (15.5-oz [439-g]) cans chickpeas (chana), rinsed and drained

Mint-cilantro chutney, for serving (page 164)

Date-tamarind chutney, for serving (page 164)

Unsweetened, plain, dairy-free yogurt, whisked, to taste, optional

Pomegranate arils, for serving, optional

Chāt masālā (homemade [page 165] or store-bought)

For the chole, heat a large pot over medium heat, and add the oil. Add the cumin seeds. When they begin to sizzle, add the onion and salt, and sauté until the onion turns slightly brown, 4 to 5 minutes. Stir in the ground coriander, chili powder, ginger, tomato paste and garam masālā, and cook for 1 minute, stirring continuously.

Add 1 cup (240 ml) water, and let the sauce simmer for 5 to 7 minutes, stirring occasionally. Stir the chickpeas into the sauce, add another 3 to 4 cups (720 to 960 ml) of water, cover, and simmer over medium heat for 30 minutes, stirring and mashing a few chickpeas occasionally. Turn off the heat.

How to Enjoy

- To serve, on a plate, arrange 2 to 3 tikkis, pour some hot chole, top with a few spoons of mint-cilantro chutney, date-tamarind chutney, unsweetened dairy-free yogurt, julienned ginger, pomegranate arils, if using, and chāt masālā.

- If entertaining, you can serve the tikkis on a platter and the chole in a large serving bowl with the toppings in several small bowls, and let the guests make their own servings to make it fun.

- Store any leftover tikkis in the refrigerator for up to a day, and reheat in the microwave. Store any leftover chole in the refrigerator for up to 2 days, and reheat in a saucepan on the stovetop.

Tips

- *Boil the potatoes in a large pot with water and salt, or use the pressure cooker.*

- *Cooling the boiled potatoes completely before shaping and frying them ensures they fry with neat edges and without breaking apart.*

- *You may make the chole first, and while it is simmering you can start the process of making the tikki.*

- *Adjust the water in the chole as needed. If it appears too thick, adjust seasoning like salt and garam masālā, and add some hot water, and simmer for a few minutes.*

Aromatic Parsi Berry Pulav

An aromatic and flavorful rice dish, layered with nuts, dried fruits and saffron

Parsi cuisine is a mixture of Indian and Persian influences and ingredients that was born because of Irani-Zorastrians who migrated to India in the early twentieth century. Berry pulav is not a common dish made in Parsi home kitchens, but actually a dish that was invented in Britannia & Co., one of Mumbai's most iconic Parsi restaurants. The distinct flavor here comes from the zereshk (barberries), which have a mildly sweet-sour flavor. It is common to substitute the zereshk with dried cranberries, as zereshk are not easily available everywhere. I am lucky to find zereshk at my local Persian store often. Tikhu-khattu-mithu (spicy, sour, sweet) is considered the holy trinity of Parsi cuisine, and you will find all those flavors in this dish. This is not a traditional recipe by any means, but it is a satisfying way to enjoy similar flavors.

Yield: 4 to 6 servings ✱ *Prep Time: 20 minutes* ✱ *Cook Time: 45 minutes*

⅓ cup (100 g) barberries (zereshk berries) or dried cranberries (see Tip)

2 pinches of saffron (kesar)

½ cup (120 ml) plain unsweetened dairy-free milk

¼ cup (60 ml) neutral oil

1 tbsp (6 g) fresh ginger, grated

4 cloves garlic, minced

1 tbsp (6 g) cumin seeds (jeera)

2 dried bay leaves (tej patta)

2 cinnamon sticks (dālchini), about 6 inches (15 cm) long

3 green cardamom pods (elaichi)

1 large red onion, thinly sliced

Salt, to taste

1 tsp ground coriander (dhaniya powder)

½ tsp red chili powder or cayenne pepper (lāl mirch powder), or according to taste

2 cups (400 g) basmati rice, rinsed and soaked for 10 minutes, drained

Unsalted toasted pistachios, for serving

Heat about ½ cup (120 ml) of water in a kettle or on the stovetop. Once it is hot, add it to a small bowl and soak the barberries for 10 minutes. Drain and set aside.

In another small bowl, soak the saffron in the milk, and set it aside.

In a large pot or Dutch oven with a lid, heat the oil over medium heat. Add the ginger and garlic, and cook for 30 seconds. Add the cumin seeds, bay leaves, cinnamon stick, cardamom pods, onion and salt, and sauté until the onion turns golden brown, 7 to 10 minutes.

Stir in the ground coriander, red chili powder, the soaked berries and the drained rice, and sauté for 2 minutes, stirring continuously. Add 3½ cups (840 ml) water, and bring the rice to a boil over medium heat.

Once you start seeing bubbles, reduce the heat, cover the pot, and let the rice cook undisturbed for 5 to 7 minutes, or until the rice has absorbed all the water. Uncover, fluff the rice using a fork, and drizzle the saffron milk over the rice. Sprinkle with unsalted toasted pistachios.

How to Enjoy

- Serve hot or at room temperature. Keep the rice covered to retain the aroma.
- Store any leftovers in the refrigerator for up to 2 days. Reheat in the microwave until heated through.
- A simple salad of raw onions and cucumbers is good on the side.

> *Tip*
> *Barberries (zereshk berries) are available in Iranian stores in most big cities. Dried cranberries are a close substitute.*

Lesser-Known Weeknight Winners

The dishes in this chapter are all my weeknight favorites and commonly eaten in most Indian homes. You will find tasty, nutritious, quick-to-prepare meals using a variety of vegetables, grains and spices. Though they are quick to make, they pack a surprising amount of flavor. I can't wait for these recipes to become a part of your weeknight dinner rotation, too!

Flavorful Pāpad ki Sabzi

Smooth and creamy yogurt-based gravy with bits of pāpad

Light-as-air pāpad is a cracker, commonly used as an accompaniment to an Indian meal. Normally you would see pāpad as supporting cast, but here it is the star of the show. Thanks to the flavors from the spices and the richness and body from the dairy-free yogurt, this recipe is perfect when you don't have vegetables on hand. The first time I had a variation of this sabzi was in Jaipur, Rajasthan. Pāpad ki sabzi was one among the many dishes on a thāli that was being served at a small home-style restaurant. They served authentic Rajasthani food—some of my favorites like dāl-baati, Rajasthani kadhi, gatte ki sabzi. But the pāpad ki sabzi stood out because of its simplicity.

Yield: 2 servings ✳ *Prep Time: 5 minutes* ✳ *Cook Time: 20 minutes*

7 to 8 pāpad (see Tips)

2 cups (480 ml) unsweetened dairy-free plain yogurt, whisked

1 tsp red chili powder (lāl mirch) or cayenne pepper

1 tsp ground ground turmeric (haldi powder)

1 tbsp (6 g) ground coriander (dhaniya powder)

¼ tsp āmchur powder (dry mango powder)

Salt, to taste

Hot water, as needed

For Tadkā (Tempering)

1 tbsp (15 ml) peanut oil or any neutral oil

2 tsp (3 g) cumin seeds (jeera)

½ tsp kalonji (nigella seeds)

⅛ tsp fenugreek seeds (methi dāna)

1 tsp fennel seeds (saunf)

1 tbsp (6 g) fresh ginger, grated

¼ tsp hing (asafoetida)

2 green chili peppers, or according to taste, split lengthwise

Roast the pāpad by following one of the methods mentioned on page 12. Roughly break each pāpad into four to six pieces. Set them aside.

Heat approximately 2 cups (480 ml) of water in a kettle or on the stovetop.

In a medium saucepan over medium-low heat, combine the yogurt, red chili powder, ground turmeric, ground coriander, āmchur powder and salt. Cook for 2 minutes, whisking often to make sure the yogurt doesn't split as it simmers.

Add about 1 cup (240 ml) of hot water, just enough to create a creamy sauce, and continue to whisk. You can add more water at a later stage if it appears too thick. Continue to simmer, and add the roasted pāpad pieces. Cook for 30 seconds, and turn off the heat. Check the consistency, and add hot water, if needed.

For the tadkā, heat the oil in a small skillet over medium-high heat for 1 minute. Once the oil is heated, add the cumin seeds. When they begin to sizzle, add the kalonji, fenugreek seeds, fennel seeds, ginger, hing and green chili peppers in quick succession, and cook for 30 seconds. Turn off heat, and add the tadkā to the sabzi. Cover immediately with a lid until ready to serve.

How to Enjoy

- This is absolutely delicious spooned over a heap of hot, steaming rice. Or pair it with Layered Triangle Parātha (page 66) or any flatbread, along with raw thinly sliced onions.

- Serve hot.

Tips

- *If you haven't shopped for pāpad before, it can be overwhelming to see a large variety of pāpad at the South Asian grocery store. For this recipe, look for udad pāpad.*

- *Storing any leftover sabzi with pāpad in it is not recommended, as the pāpad thickens the gravy.*

Mouthwatering Pānch Phoran Dāl

Red lentils with five-spice tempering

Dāl is both an ingredient (when we are referring to lentils/pulses) and a dish (when we are referring to the stew). There are numerous ways to prepare the many dāls of Indian cuisine, but this one is special because of the tadkā (tempering) with the five spices called pānch phoran, commonly found in East Indian dishes. Pānch phoran refers to a blend of whole cumin seeds, black mustard seeds, fenugreek seeds, nigella seeds and fennel seeds. This tadkā gives the dāl a very exotic taste.

Yield: 2 to 3 servings when served with rice ✳ *Prep Time: 10 minutes* ✳ *Cook Time: about 45 minutes*

1 cup (192 g) masoor dāl (split red lentils)

1 tsp salt, or to taste

½ tsp ground turmeric (haldi powder)

For Tadkā (Tempering)

1 tsp neutral oil

2 chili peppers, or to taste, finely chopped

4 cloves garlic, minced

A few fresh curry leaves (kadi patta), optional

1 tbsp (7 g) pānch phoran blend

Finely chopped fresh cilantro, for serving

1 to 2 tbsp (15 to 30 ml) fresh lemon juice, for serving

Tip

Make sure you are simmering the dāl on low. Low and slow will naturally break down the dāl and give it the perfect comforting consistency. Check the quantity of water often, and feel free to add hot water, if needed, at any point while the lentils are simmering.

Give the lentils a good rinse in a colander. You can do this by placing the lentils in a colander under running water, and then scooping up handfuls of the lentils and scrubbing them with your hands. Masoor dāl is usually dusty, and the water will turn milky very quickly when you start rinsing them. After a thorough scrubbing, drain off the water, refill with clean water, and repeat this process until the water runs clear.

Transfer the lentils to a deep saucepan, add about 3 cups (720 ml) of water, the salt and ground turmeric, and bring to a boil. Once the lentils begin to boil, reduce the heat and let it simmer gently, stirring occasionally. You may skim the foam that rises to the top with a ladle and discard it.

Continue cooking the lentils, stirring often, until they look like they can easily be mashed, adding hot water as needed, 20 to 30 minutes depending on the age of the lentils. Once the lentils are cooked, mix everything together using a whisk. The whisk helps to break down the lentils further and give body to the dāl. Reduce the heat to its lowest setting.

Heat a tadkā pan or skillet. Add the oil, and allow it to warm. Add the chili peppers and garlic, and toss with a spoon. After 10 seconds, add the curry leaves, if using, followed by the pānch phoran blend. Toast for a minute, stirring with a spoon to make sure the spices don't burn. Turn off the heat, and pour the tadkā onto the dāl. Immediately cover the dāl with a lid, and turn off heat.

Add the fresh cilantro and lemon juice before serving. The lemon juice adds a lot of freshness here.

How to Enjoy

- For a complete meal, serve hot with rice or Layered Triangle Parātha (page 66) or any flatbread with Sweet-and-Spicy Shakarkand Bhujiya (page 122) and some pappadām on the side.

- Store any leftover dāl in the refrigerator for up to a day, but dāl is best when eaten fresh. Reheating dāl doesn't taste as good as when it is made fresh, but the best way to reheat is on the stovetop. You may need to add some hot boiling water into the dāl because refrigeration causes the dāl to thicken.

Fuss-Free Mirch Bhopli

Stir-fried bell peppers coated in a spiced-chickpea flour paste

This dish is straightforward, easy to make, a lunch box staple in my house and my husband's favorite. If you ask me to pick a perfect weeknight low-effort meal, it will be this sabzi with roti (flatbread) and dāl. It is my quick version of the humble zunkā, a chickpea flour dish traditionally served with bhākri (flatbread). While this flavorful dish is packed with several spices, the crunchy texture and taste of the bell peppers still shine through.

*Yield: 6 servings * Prep Time: 7 minutes * Cook Time: 20 minutes*

3 tbsp (45 ml) neutral oil

2 tsp (6 g) black mustard seeds (rāi)

1 tbsp (6 g) cumin seeds (jeera)

¼ tsp hing (asafoetida)

4 large, firm green bell peppers, diced

Salt, to taste

1 tsp Kashmiri red chili powder

1 tsp ground turmeric (haldi powder)

½ tsp ground fennel (saunf powder)

1 tbsp (6 g) ground coriander (dhaniya powder)

1 tsp granulated sugar

4 tbsp (20 g) besan (chickpea/gram flour)

¾ tsp āmchur powder (dry mango powder)

Roasted unsalted peanuts, coarsely chopped, optional

Heat the oil in a large, non-stick skillet over medium heat. Add the black mustard seeds, and toast them until they start to pop, about 1 minute. Add the cumin seeds, and once they begin to sizzle, reduce the heat to low. Add the hing, bell peppers, salt, Kashmiri red chili powder, ground turmeric, ground fennel and ground coriander, and mix well to combine.

Increase the heat to medium, sprinkle a few drops of water into the skillet, and continue to cook the bell pepper for 5 to 7 minutes, stirring occasionally. The bell peppers should be crisp-tender, not soft.

Stir in the sugar, reduce the heat once again, add the besan, the āmchur and about 2 tablespoons (30 ml) of water and mix them well to coat the peppers with the besan. Continue to cook for another 5 to 7 minutes, stirring occasionally, making sure the besan doesn't burn. You want to cook the besan for a few minutes so that it loses its rawness.

Turn off the heat, and stir in the peanuts, if using. Check for seasonings, and make sure the besan is cooked. Adjust seasonings, as needed.

How to Enjoy

- This tastes great with Layered Triangle Parātha (page 66) or any flatbread, or as a side dish for rice and Mouthwatering Pānch Phoran Dāl (page 46).

- Any leftovers can be stored in the refrigerator for up to 2 days, although it tastes best on the day it is cooked.

- To reheat, microwave the sabzi at 30-second intervals or on the stovetop, making sure not to overcook the bell peppers.

Tip

This sabzi can be ruined due to some common mistakes. It can get burned easily because it is a dry stir-fry. Make sure you are stirring often and watching it while it is cooking. The other common mistake is not giving enough time for the besan to cook. Give it some time, at least 5 to 7 minutes, while stirring often. Also, do not overcook the bell peppers.

Crispy Adai

Nutrient-dense savory lentil pancakes

The word adai, for me, is synonymous with easy deliciousness. Adai (pronounced "uh-dei") is nutritious, filling and an easy dish for any meal of the day. As a child, I did not like adai, but I later came to appreciate its unique texture and convenient preparation. Adai batter is commonly found in Tamil homes premade and ready to be converted into a nutritious meal.

Yield: 12 to 15 adais ✳ Prep Time: 15 minutes ✳ Cook Time: 5 to 7 minutes per adai (plus soaking time)

For the Adai (see Tips)

2 cups (400 g) raw uncooked rice, rinsed and then soaked for at least 3 hours

½ cup (100 g) chana dāl (dalia or roasted split chickpeas)

½ cup (100 g) toor dāl (split pigeon peas)

¼ cup (55 g) urad dāl (split black gram)

1 to 2 green chili peppers, or according to taste

4 whole dried red chilis, or according to taste

¼ tsp hing (asafoetida)

Salt, to taste

Handful of fresh cilantro, finely chopped, optional

5 to 7 fresh curry leaves, roughly chopped, optional

Gingelly oil, for cooking (see Tips)

To make the adai, drain the rice and add it into a blender along with 1 cup (240 ml) of filtered water, and blend until smooth. You may add a few more spoonfuls of water to help the blender, if needed, but avoid adding too much as that will cause the rice not to process smoothly. Pour the batter into a large mixing bowl, and set aside.

Drain the water from the chana dāl, toor dāl and urad dāl, and add them to the blender along with the green chili peppers, whole dried red chilies, hing and salt. To the blender, add approximately ¼ cup (60 ml) of water and blend the mixture coarsely. Stir the ground dāl mixture into the ground rice. Add the fresh cilantro and curry leaves, if using, and thoroughly mix the batter. The consistency should be like pancake batter, but the texture should be coarse.

Heat a well-seasoned cast-iron skillet or nonstick pan over medium heat. Grease the surface lightly with oil.

Sprinkle a few drops of water on the hot skillet—it is ready when the drops of water sizzle and evaporate right away. Give the batter a stir, and ladle ½ cup (80 g) onto the skillet.

Use the back of the ladle to evenly spread the batter in a circle.

Create a little hole in the center of the adai, and drizzle some oil all around it. Let it cook for a minute, and carefully flip the adai using a flat spatula, making sure the bottom is cooked before flipping. Cook the other side, another 3 minutes, by pressing it down onto the skillet using the spatula. The adai tastes better when both sides are crisp and brown. Transfer the adai to a plate, and repeat with the remaining batter.

(continued)

Crispy Adai *(continued)*

How to Enjoy

- Serve hot with these commonly-paired accompaniments: Coconut Chutney (page 111), Robust Kadala Curry (page 59), molagapodi (also known as chutney podi, which can be found in most South Asian stores) or jaggery.

- Store any remaining batter covered in the refrigerator for up to 2 days. Stir the batter thoroughly before use.

Tips

- *I like to use raw idli rice for adai, but really any variety like long-grain or short-grain would work.*

- *Soak the lentils for just 20 minutes before you prepare the batter. You want the texture of the batter to be coarse. Soaking the lentils for too long before blending/grinding will make the batter too smooth.*

- *Gingelly oil is widely used in South Indian cooking. You can find it in well-stocked South Asian grocery stores. If you do not have access to it, use any neutral oil of your choice.*

Scrumptious Dum Aloo Kashmiri

Fried baby potatoes slow cooked in aromatic spices

This is my take on a classic Kashmiri dish. The big, bold flavor is a result of dum cooking, the process of slow cooking the ingredients in a tightly sealed, heavy-bottomed pot to let the dish breathe in its own aroma. Some variations of this dish include the use of plain yogurt to create a creamy spiced sauce as the base. I borrowed this idea from a Kashmiri friend, who shared that she grew up eating dum aloo sans yogurt and that the main flavor here comes from the spices commonly used in Kashmiri cuisine, like fennel and ground dried ginger.

Yield: 4 servings ✳ Prep Time: 20 minutes ✳ Cook Time: 50 minutes

1 lb (454 g) medium-sized baby potatoes

Salt, to taste

6 tbsp (90 ml) mustard oil or neutral oil (see Tips)

2 tbsp (12 g) cumin seeds (jeera)

1 medium-sized cinnamon stick (dālchini), coarsely crushed

2 green cardamom pods, coarsely crushed

2 bay leaves (tej patta)

2 whole cloves (lavang)

1 tbsp (6 g) Kashmiri chili powder

1 tbsp (5 g) ground fennel (saunf powder)

½ tsp ground turmeric (haldi powder)

1 tsp hing (asafoetida)

1 tsp ground dried ginger

Place the baby potatoes in a large pot and add enough water to cover them. Season with salt. Cook them until they are fork tender but still holding shape, about 7 to 10 minutes. Drain the potatoes in a colander and set them aside to cool.

Once you are able to comfortably touch the potatoes, peel the skin off (you should be able to easily pull it off with your hands). Using a toothpick, prick the potatoes all over and set the potatoes aside.

Heat the oil in a deep, medium-sized, heavy-bottomed wok over medium-low heat until shimmering. Add the potatoes into the oil and fry them, stirring often, until they are reasonably golden-brown all over, about 7 to 10 minutes. Using a slotted spoon, remove the potatoes from the wok and transfer them onto a plate lined with paper towel.

Reheat the wok with the oil over medium heat. To the same wok, add the cumin seeds, crushed cinnamon sticks, crushed cardamom pods, bay leaves and whole cloves, then toast the spices until fragrant, about 1 minute.

Reduce the heat to the lowest setting. Meanwhile, in a bowl, mix together the Kashmiri chili powder, ground fennel, ground turmeric, hing and ground dried ginger, along with ⅓ cup (80 ml) of water.

Add the spice mixture to the wok. Cook over low heat for 2 minutes, or until fragrant, stirring frequently, making sure the spices don't burn. Add the fried potatoes, season with salt, then stir to coat the potatoes with the spice mixture.

(continued)

Fresh cilantro, to taste

Add hot water, just enough to cover the surface of the potatoes. Cover with a heavy lid immediately afterwards, then place a heavy object on top of the lid and simmer on low heat for around 20 minutes (this cooking process is called "dum"). The sauce should have reduced and will appear lightly saucy.

Uncover the pot and check for seasoning and consistency. Adjust if needed. Stir in the cilantro.

How to Enjoy

Serve with Layered Triangle Parātha (page 66) or white rice along with Raita (page 165).

Tips

- *Cook the potatoes undisturbed for 20 minutes to let the flavors infuse and permeate through the potatoes.*
- *Mustard oil is the preferred cooking oil here. If you are unable to find it or find its taste too pungent, use any neutral oil.*

Colorful Vegetable Sabzi

Mixed vegetable gravy with simple spices

There are many mixed vegetable sabzis common in India, some are especially popular in restaurants—veg Kolhapuri (where the spices used in the base sauce are local to Kolhapur) and veg Jaipuri (where the spices are local to Jaipur). My dad's favorite sabzi to order at restaurants is veg achaari—another sabzi with a medley of vegetables and pickling spices. This home-style version gives you the best of both worlds.

Yield: 4 to 6 servings ✳ *Prep Time: 15 minutes* ✳ *Cook Time: about 45 minutes*

1 medium head cauliflower, cut into florets

1 large potato, peeled and cut into medium cubes

Salt, to taste

2 tsp (10 ml) neutral oil

1 tbsp (6 g) cumin seeds (jeera)

1 tbsp (6 g) fresh ginger, grated

3 cloves garlic, minced

1 green chili pepper, or according to taste, finely chopped

1 medium red onion, thinly sliced

2 medium tomatoes, diced

1 tsp ground turmeric (haldi powder)

2 tbsp (12 g) ground coriander (dhaniya powder)

1 tsp Kashmiri red chili powder, or according to taste

1 large carrot, peeled and diced

1 cup (100 g) green beans, ends trimmed off and cut into thirds

½ cup (70 g) frozen green peas

2 tsp (4 g) garam masālā (homemade [see page 165] or store-bought)

1 tbsp (4 g) kasuri methi (dry fenugreek leaves)

Chopped fresh cilantro, for serving

Set a colander in the sink to drain the cauliflower and the potatoes in the next step.

Bring a large pot of water to a boil, and add the cauliflower, potatoes and salt. Cook for 4 minutes, until the cauliflower and potatoes are slightly tender but still hold the shape. Drain them into the colander, and add them into the pot. Cover to retain the heat.

Heat a skillet over medium heat, and then add the oil and the cumin seeds. When the cumin seeds begin to sizzle, about 30 seconds, add the ginger, garlic and the green chili pepper. Cook until fragrant, about 30 seconds, and add the onion. Season with salt, and cook until the onion turns light brown, 2 to 3 minutes. Stir in the tomatoes, ground turmeric, ground coriander and Kashmiri red chili powder, and continue to cook until the tomatoes turn soft, about 2 minutes.

Add about ½ cup (120 ml) water, followed by the carrot, green beans and green peas. Cover the skillet, and cook over medium heat, stirring occasionally, for 7 to 10 minutes, or until the vegetables are cooked through but still hold their shape.

Turn off the heat. Adjust water and seasonings, if needed. If the gravy appears too dry, you can add some hot water and mix well. Add the garam masālā and kasuri methi. Sprinkle with the fresh cilantro just before serving.

How to Enjoy

- Serve hot with Layered Triangle Parātha (page 66), Raita (page 165) and thinly sliced raw onions. If the sabzi is thin, it can be paired with rice as well.

- To reheat, simmer the sabzi and a few spoonfuls of hot water in a saucepan.

Tips

- *Fresh vegetables (except the frozen peas) are recommended. If you are in a pinch, feel free to use frozen mixed vegetables. Follow the above steps until you add the Kashmiri red chili powder, then add the frozen vegetables, and follow the remaining instructions. Cooking times will vary.*

- *The consistency of the sabzi and the doneness of the vegetables is your preference. If you like them mushier, cook them for a little longer.*

Robust Kadala Curry

Kerala black chickpea curry

During my childhood, weekends always began with me waking up to the aroma of coconut oil, curry leaves and roasted spices from the puttu and kadala curry being prepared by my parents for brunch. Kadala curry is a black chickpea stew cooked in a freshly ground, spicy base. The Kerala garam masālā used here is so flavorful. The process of roasting the spices, called varatu aracha in Malayalam, is what truly elevates this dish. It is typically served with puttu, which is a soft, steamed cylinder of ground rice—a savory dish, perfect to soak up all the flavors of the kadala curry. Kadala curry is also often paired with rice and other rice-based dishes of southern India. Yes, this comes with a long list of spices, but every single one is worth it.

Yield: 4 to 6 servings ✳ *Prep Time: 10 minutes, plus soaking time* ✳ *Cook Time: 1 hour*

8 oz (226 g) kāla chana (black chickpeas), soaked in water for at least 6 to 8 hours (see Tips)

Salt, to taste

4 tbsp (20 g) coconut (fresh or frozen) (see Tips)

½ tsp fennel seeds (saunf)

2 whole cloves (lavang)

2 (1-inch [2.5-cm]) cinnamon sticks (dālchini)

7 to 10 black peppercorns (kāli mirch)

1 whole mace (jāvitri)

1 tsp Kashmiri red chili powder

2 tsp (4 g) ground coriander (dhaniya powder)

Pinch of ground nutmeg (jaiphal)

In an electric pressure cooker, add the kāla chana to the inner pot. Add 3 cups (720 ml) water and a pinch of salt, and cook on high pressure for 20 minutes. Let the pressure release naturally.

Keep a medium plate readily accessible to transfer the contents of the skillet in the following step.

While the kāla chana are cooking, heat a small skillet over medium heat. Dry-roast the coconut in the skillet, stirring continuously, until light brown, for 5 minutes (see Tips). Transfer the roasted coconut to the plate.

To the same skillet, add the fennel seeds, whole cloves, cinnamon sticks, black peppercorns and whole mace, and roast them until fragrant, 3 to 4 minutes, stirring continuously.

Transfer the roasted whole spices to the plate with the coconut. Reduce the heat to low, add the Kashmiri red chili powder, ground coriander and ground nutmeg to the skillet, and toast the ground spices for 1 minute, stirring continuously.

Transfer the toasted ground spices to the plate. Put the roasted coconut and the spices into a blender with ¼ cup (60 ml) water, and process them to make a masālā paste. Set it aside.

Once the pressure is released, drain the kāla chana into a colander. Reserve the water in which the kāla chana were cooked.

(continued)

Robust Kadala Curry *(continued)*

1 tbsp (14 g) coconut oil

1 tsp black mustard seeds (rāi)

7 to 10 fresh curry leaves (kadi patta) (see Tips)

2 green chili peppers, or according to taste

1 tbsp (6 g) fresh ginger, grated

1 medium red onion, chopped

2 medium tomatoes, finely chopped or pureed (about 1½ cups [200 g])

1 tsp ground turmeric (haldi powder)

¼ cup (60 ml) coconut milk

Handful of fresh cilantro, chopped, for serving, optional

Heat a large saucepan or the pressure cooker pot over medium heat. Add the coconut oil and, once it starts shimmering, add the mustard seeds. Once the mustard seeds begin to pop, carefully add the curry leaves, followed by the green chili peppers and ginger, and cook for 30 seconds. Stir in the onion, season with salt, and continue to cook, stirring often, until the onion turns pink, 2 minutes.

Stir in the tomatoes, ground turmeric, 1 cup (240 ml) of water and the reserved cooking water, and cook over medium heat until the tomatoes are cooked, 3 to 4 minutes.

Add the ground masālā paste and the cooked kāla chana, and simmer on low for 10 minutes, stirring occasionally. You may add more water, about ½ to ¾ cup (120 to 180 ml), to adjust the consistency at this point.

Check for seasoning, and stir in the coconut milk. Garnish with cilantro, if using.

How to Enjoy

Serve hot with rice and pappadām. It also pairs well with Crispy Adai (page 50).

Tips

- To speed up the soaking process, you can soak the kāla chana in hot water for 3 hours instead.

- If using frozen coconut, remember to thaw a portion for this recipe at least 30 minutes before roasting, or microwave the frozen coconut for faster thawing.

- Fresh curry leaves are available in well-stocked South Asian stores. There is no substitute.

Zesty Kadhai Tofu

Tofu and bell peppers cooked in a spicy masālā

Kadhai tofu is a veganized version of kadhai paneer. This is the first tofu dish I prepared when I wanted to re-create a paneer dish when I started eating plant-based. I was pleasantly surprised by the result. I did not miss the paneer at all, as the tofu absorbed all the flavors from the kadhai masālā (kadhai means "wok" or "skillet with sloping sides" and masālā means "a blend of spices"), tomatoes, onions and aromatics just like paneer would. The recipe is divided into three main steps. First, toss the tofu cubes in corn flour and then crisping them up in a skillet. Next, make the fresh kadhai masālā. Finally, combine the two, and add some fresh vegetables and aromatics to make the gravy and complete the dish.

Serves: 4 ✳ Prep Time: 10 minutes ✳ Cook Time: 60 minutes

For the Kadhai Masālā

1 to 2 whole dry Kashmiri red chili peppers

2 tsp (4 g) fennel seeds (saunf)

6 black peppercorns (kāli mirch)

2 tsp (3 g) cumin seeds (jeera)

1 tbsp (5 g) coriander seeds (dhaniya)

For the Tofu

1 block extra-firm or super-firm tofu, drained, pressed and cut into cubes

3 tbsp (25 g) cornstarch

2 tbsp (30 ml) neutral oil

To make the kadhai masālā, in a small skillet over medium heat, toast the whole dry Kashmiri red chili pepper, fennel seeds, black peppercorns, cumin seeds and coriander seeds until fragrant, 3 to 4 minutes, stirring continuously. Turn off the heat, and set aside to cool for 5 minutes. Transfer the toasted spices to a spice grinder or a mortar and pestle, and grind to a coarse powder.

To shallow-fry the tofu, to a medium bowl, add the tofu, and sprinkle with the cornstarch. Gently give the tofu cubes a mix by tossing them in the bowl to make sure they are evenly coated in the flour. Set the tofu aside.

To a large skillet over medium heat, add the oil. While the oil is heating, place a plate next to the skillet for the fried tofu cubes. Carefully place the tofu in the skillet using your hands or a pair of tongs. Cook the tofu on all sides until they appear light brown, 7 to 10 minutes. Remove the tofu from the pan using a slotted spoon, and place it on the plate.

(continued)

For the Gravy

1 tbsp (15 ml) neutral oil

1 tbsp (6 g) cumin seeds (jeera)

3 cloves garlic, minced

1 tbsp (6 g) fresh ginger, grated

1 large red onion, chopped

5 medium tomatoes, finely chopped

1 large bell pepper, finely diced

Salt, to taste

1 tsp ground turmeric (haldi powder)

1 tsp Kashmiri red chili powder, or according to taste

2 medium green bell peppers, diced into roughly the same size as the tofu

1 large white onion, chopped into roughly same size the as tofu, layers separated

2 tsp (4 g) garam masālā (homemade [see page 165] or store-bought)

1 tbsp (4 g) kasuri methi (dry fenugreek leaves)

Chopped fresh cilantro

Cashew cream (page 164) or store-bought dairy-free cream, optional

For the gravy, to the same skillet, add the oil. Add the cumin seeds, and cook until fragrant, about 30 seconds. Add the garlic, ginger and red onion, and sauté until the onion turns light brown, 4 minutes. Add the tomatoes, finely diced bell pepper, salt, ground turmeric and Kashmiri red chili powder, and cook until the tomatoes soften, creating a sauce, 4 to 5 minutes. If the mixture appears dry, add a few drops of water to help the tomatoes continue cooking.

Add the green bell peppers and white onion, and cook for 2 minutes, stirring continuously. The peppers and the onions don't need to cook for too long, as they should retain some crunch.

Stir in the fried tofu. Reduce the heat to low, and cook for another 3 to 5 minutes, making sure the tofu cubes are coated in the sauce, then increase the heat, and stir-fry until the vegetables appear charred, about 3 minutes.

Sprinkle with the garam masālā, kasuri methi (crush them between your palms while adding them) and fresh cilantro. Turn off the heat. Check for seasoning, and adjust accordingly. Serve with cashew cream or dairy-free cream, if using.

How to Enjoy

- Serve hot with any store-bought flatbread, Layered Triangle Parātha (page 66) or rice.

- Store any leftovers in airtight container in the refrigerator for up to 2 days.

- To reheat, add the sabzi to a hot kadhai, and toss for 3 to 5 minutes, or heat in the microwave. If the sabzi appears dry, sprinkle a few drops of water before reheating.

Smoky Baingan Bharta

Roasted, spiced eggplant mash

As a child, I remember telling my mom I could never eat the dish she was going to prepare, after seeing her roasting a large, glossy eggplant over a stove flame. I refused to even give it a try. Until one day, when my ammamma (maternal grandma) made the same thing. She made the bharta in an iron kadhai (wok), transferred it to a serving bowl, and then added some leftover rice to the kadhai and gave it a toss to combine the rice with the flavorful browned bits still left in it. At that moment, I wanted to give it a try. The rice had taken on a delicious flavor—the sweetness of onions, the tanginess of tomatoes, the smokiness of the roasted eggplant and, of course, ammamma's touch—they all worked together so well. I realized that roasting eggplant gives it an incredible depth of flavor. As an adult, I have acquired quite a taste for it. I wish I had tried it sooner.

*Yield: 4 servings * Prep Time: 10 minutes * Cook Time: about 1 hour (including roasting time)*

1 large eggplant, about 1½ lb (680 g)

4 to 5 cloves garlic, peeled

1 tsp neutral oil or mustard oil, plus more for brushing eggplant

1 tsp fresh ginger, grated

1 medium red onion, finely chopped

1 green chili pepper, or accordingly to taste, finely chopped

2 small tomatoes, finely diced

1 tsp salt, or to taste

¼ tsp red chili powder (lāl mirch) or cayenne pepper

1½ tsp (3 g) ground coriander (dhaniya powder)

Pinch of ground turmeric (haldi powder)

Finely chopped fresh cilantro

Tip
The best flavor comes out when you roast the eggplant on an open flame. Give it time and be patient when roasting, and make sure you are turning it every few minutes so there is even charring on the exterior. I use a roti grill that is set over the stovetop.

Before you begin roasting the eggplant, set a bowl with a lid nearby for the roasted eggplant.

Using a paring knife, make three to four vertical incisions lengthwise, from stem to end, on the eggplant, and insert the garlic cloves.

Brush some mustard oil over the eggplant, and lay the eggplant on the flame of the stove, or on a barbecue (see Tip). Roast until the eggplant is very soft and black, turning regularly with the help of tongs to ensure it cooks evenly.

Once the eggplant is blackened all over and soft within, transfer it to the bowl to cool. The eggplant needs to be soft enough to mash with a fork or spoon and blackened and blistered on the outside. Cover the eggplant for about 5 minutes.

Scoop the eggplant flesh out of the skin using a spoon, or you can peel the skin off the eggplant using your fingers. It is OK to leave a few flecks of the eggplant skin. Roughly mash the eggplant flesh and the garlic with a fork and set aside.

Meanwhile, heat 1 teaspoon of the oil in a skillet over medium heat. Add the ginger, and cook for about 10 seconds. Add the onion and chili pepper, and sauté until the onion turns pink, about 3 minutes, stirring frequently. Add the tomatoes, salt, red chili powder, ground coriander and ground turmeric, and cook until the onion and tomatoes are soft and limp, 4 to 5 minutes, stirring frequently.

Stir in the mashed eggplant and garlic mixture, cover, and cook for about 15 minutes on low heat, stirring occasionally. Turn off the heat. Taste and adjust seasoning, if needed. Add fresh cilantro just before serving.

How to Enjoy
Serve with any hot flatbread like Layered Triangle Parātha (page 66), roti or rice.

Layered Triangle Parātha

Simple whole wheat layered flatbread

When I was about 6 years old, my friends and I played a word-clue game where you clue a certain word to your teammate by saying another word that is related to it. The word I had to clue was "triangle," and my clue to my teammate was "parātha." Nobody could guess the answer, but when I explained that in my house we only ate parāthas that were triangle in shape, everyone had a hearty laugh. Parātha is a layered-dough flatbread. My mom would make the plain version to be paired with subzis and gravies, and a sweet version, too, with sugar or sometimes jaggery stuffed inside. It always brings back sweet memories of my ammamma and the rural charm of her sitting on a woven, backless bench on the outdoor porch of her home backyard and patiently, tirelessly and effortlessly, making parāthas on a chulha (woodfire stove) for all of us whenever we we visited my grandparents.. This parātha is a treasured staple.

*Yield: 6 parāthas * Prep Time: 20 minutes * Cook Time: 25 minutes*

1½ cups (180 g) whole wheat flour (gchun ka āta/durum āta)

Pinch of salt

¾ cup (180 ml) warm water

Neutral oil, for brushing

In a large mixing bowl, add the flour, salt and water. Knead the dough for about 5 minutes, adding more water, a little at a time, if necessary, to make a pliable dough. Cover and rest the dough for 15 minutes.

Take a golf-sized ball from the dough, and using a rolling pin, roll it into a small disc, about 5 inches (13 cm) in diameter. Brush some oil on the surface of the dough, and fold the circle into a semicircle. Fold the semicircle once again to form a triangle. Dust with flour and roll out evenly, while rotating the triangle after a few rolls. Keep doing this process, until the triangle is about 7 inches (18 cm) long.

Heat a nonstick skillet over medium-high heat, and once it is hot, place the rolled parātha dough in the skillet. Cook for about 30 seconds, flip the parātha using a flat-head spatula, and cook for another 30 seconds. Flip again, brush the parātha with some oil, press it down with the spatula, and allow it to rise and puff up. Flip and cook until it gets golden with brown spots all over.

How to Enjoy

- Serve hot or at room temperature with sabzis, Raita (page 165) or as wraps.
- Store any leftovers in an airtight container for up to 2 days. To reheat, preheat a tavā or skillet, and cook the parāthas on both sides.

Tip

You can find gehun ka āta (whole wheat flour) at all South Asian grocery stores.

Most-Loved Comfort Food

In this chapter, you will find dishes brimming with coziness and comfort. It is hard to pick a favorite here because each dish evokes a sense of nostalgia for me. That is what comfort food is all about, right? It reminds you of home. But even if you did not grow up eating any of these dishes, they are sure to warm and comfort you because they are all made with love and meant to nourish the spirit.

Wholesome Rājma Masāla

Spiced kidney bean stew

Aaah. The simple joys of eating perfectly cooked basmati rice with creamy rājma masālā poured over the top, topped with thinly sliced raw onions. This is my daughter's favorite comfort food. Soft, almost melt-in-your-mouth kidney beans are cooked in a spiced onion-tomato base, which sounds basic, but when properly cooked, the soft kidney beans absorb all those flavors. I encourage you to use dried kidney beans for this recipe instead of canned ones. A soft and creamy texture is important for rājma, and canned beans cannot give you the perfect creaminess. The flavor and the color of the cooking water from the beans is something I love and believe is important in creating a beautiful, dreamy consistency, which helps coat every grain of rice.

Yield: 4 to 6 servings ✳ *Prep Time: 20 minutes (plus soaking time)* ✳ *Cook Time: 1 hour*

1½ cups (270 g) dried kidney beans (rājma)

4 tbsp (60 ml) neutral oil

1 large red onion, thinly sliced

Salt, to taste

1 tbsp (6 g) fresh ginger, grated

4 cloves garlic, peeled

1 cup (240 ml) tomato puree (see Tips)

1 tbsp (6 g) ground coriander (dhaniya powder)

2 tsp red chili powder (lāl mirch) or cayenne pepper, or according to taste

1 tsp garam masālā (homemade [see page 165] or store-bought)

Rinse the kidney beans under running water thoroughly, and soak them in water for about 6 hours (see Tips).

Drain the water, transfer the kidney beans to a pressure cooker, and add enough fresh, cold water to cover 2 inches (5 cm) above the surface of the beans. Pressure-cook the beans until they are tender and somewhat hold their shape.

Line a plate with a paper towel, and set aside.

In a large saucepan, add the oil, and heat it over medium heat until shimmering. Add the onion, season with salt, and fry until the onion is golden brown, stirring often, 7 to 10 minutes. Turn off the heat. Using a slotted spoon, transfer the onion to the plate lined with paper towel.

In a blender, add the browned onion, the ginger and garlic, and blend to a smooth paste. You may add a few spoonfuls of water if needed for consistency. Set the paste aside.

In the same saucepan, heat the remaining oil. Add the tomato puree, ground coriander, red chili powder and garam masālā and cook for 5 minutes to get rid of the raw tomato taste. Add the onion paste to the saucepan, and simmer the sauce for about 15 minutes.

Stir in the cooked kidney beans along with some of the cooking liquid or hot boiling water, enough to reach your desired consistency.

(continued)

2 tsp (1 g) kasuri methi (dry fenugreek leaves) (see Tips)

Finely chopped fresh cilantro

Simmer the beans in the masālā sauce for 15 minutes, uncovered, over low heat; this allows the spices to release all their flavors and get into the tender kidney beans. Crush the kasuri methi, and add it to the bean mixture. Check for seasoning, add salt, and adjust other spices, if needed. Turn off the heat, and sprinkle with the cilantro.

How to Enjoy

- You can use any grain of choice to serve with rājma but white basmati rice and rājma masālā with sliced raw onions on the side is the classic combination.

- Serve with a spoon, or eat the rājma with some rice (see Tips) by hand.

Tips

- *You can buy canned tomato puree, or make your own by blending 3 fresh ripe tomatoes, then straining any pulp and seeds.*

- *To reduce the soaking time of the beans, soak them in hot boiling water for 2 hours.*

- *Kasuri methi adds a lot of depth and flavor to sabzis and gravies, especially Punjabi ones. Look for it in the spice aisle.*

- *Dry rājma is sold in most well-stocked grocery stores in the dry lentils and beans aisle. Light or dark red kidney beans are the same. You may use either of them.*

Minty Rasam

Spicy, sour, minty soup

My thatha (maternal grandfather) always called this dish "gold coin rasam" because of the shiny specks of oil floating on top from the final tadkā (tempering). Rasam is a piquant, soupy broth, typically made with thinned-out lentil water, with characteristic flavors from souring agents and ground spices (called rasam podi in Tamil). If you ask Indians from the southern part of the country what their idea of comfort food is, their answer would probably be rasam. It has different names in different parts of southern India, like Chaaru, Saru, etc. Of course, there are different regional interpretations of this dish as well. Some are thicker, some are more sour, and some are made plain and light, without any lentil water. Rasam is usually served with rice, but it can be served as a soup as well. It is common for people to skip the rice and only have rasam when they are too full to eat a meal. It is also common to have just a few spoons of rice and several ladles of piping-hot rasam poured over it when someone is nursing a cold or during convalescence.

*Yield: 4 servings when served with rice * Prep Time: 10 minutes * Cook Time: 40 minutes*

1 medium tomato, diced

½ tsp ground turmeric (haldi powder)

2 green chili peppers, or according to taste, split in half lengthwise

¾ cup (18 g) fresh mint leaves, finely chopped, divided

½ cup (100 g) dry toor dāl (split pigeon peas)

1 tbsp (5 g) coriander seeds (dhaniya)

1 tsp cumin seeds (jeera)

1 tsp black peppercorns (kāli mirch)

Salt, to taste

½ tsp granulated sugar

Boil about 3 to 4 cups (720 to 960 ml) of water in a kettle or a saucepan before you begin the cooking process. You will be using this in the next few steps.

In a medium saucepan, combine the tomato, about 2½ cups (600 ml) of the boiling water, the ground turmeric, green chili pepper, and ½ cup (12 g) of the mint leaves. Bring the mixture to a gentle simmer over medium heat.

Meanwhile, in a small skillet, dry-roast the toor dāl, coriander seeds, cumin seeds and black peppercorns for 3 to 4 minutes, stirring often. Once the toor dāl and spices appear toasted and are fragrant, set them aside to cool for about 5 minutes.

If the water in the saucepan has evaporated during this time, add ¼ cup (60 ml) of hot water, and continue to simmer.

Grind the cooled and roasted toor dāl and spices in a spice grinder. Add the freshly ground spices to the saucepan, and continue to simmer.

Add 3 cups (720 ml) of the hot water, the salt and sugar, and bring to a gentle simmer. Do not boil. Once you start seeing the surface of the rasam getting frothy and rising to the top of the saucepan, turn off the heat. If you can time the tadkā (tempering) right when the rasam rises to the top of the pan, the flavor gets even better. If not, finish this step, turn off heat, and move on to the tadkā (tempering) step.

(continued)

Minty Rasam (continued)

2 tsp (10 ml) neutral oil

1 tsp mustard seeds (rāi)

Pinch of hing (asafoetida)

3 to 4 fresh curry leaves

3 tbsp (45 ml) fresh lemon juice

For the tadkā, heat a small skillet with the oil. Add the mustard seeds, and once they begin to pop, gently add the hing and fresh curry leaves. Turn off heat, and pour it into the rasam. Immediately stir in the remaining ¼ cup (7 g) of fresh mint and the lemon juice, and cover the saucepan to retain all the flavors.

How to Enjoy

- Serve the rasam as a soup in small cups or with rice. For a complete meal, add some white rice to a plate, and pour piping-hot rasam on top of the rice. Serve rice and rasam with Earthy Beet Poriyal (page 121).

- You can also serve rasam as an appetizer in the winter months. Serve hot in individual cups or soup bowls, topped with fresh mint.

- Leftover rasam can be refrigerated for up to 2 days. To reheat, simply simmer the rasam in a saucepan. For added freshness, sprinkle some freshly ground black pepper and/or freshly chopped mint or cilantro on the reheated rasam.

Tips

- *You can cook the toor dāl in the pressure cooker as well. Cook it as directed above in the pressure cooker instead of the stovetop, and then continue with the recipe as directed.*

- *You can find packs of toor dāl at your local South Asian grocery store in different sizes in the aisle with lentils. Dāls/lentils have a long shelf life. You can buy a regular-sized pack and store them in a dry place in an airtight container.*

Hearty Vegetable Ishtoo

Malabar coconut milk vegetable stew

Kerala prides itself in being the hub of the spice trade in India and has maintained this distinction for thousands of years. This simple stew is made with a combination of aromatics and spices that are native to Kerala. The vegetables are simmered in the spicy coconut milk mixture until they become tender. The first time I had this dish was when my ammamma made it, and I remember being totally shocked that such a flavorful dish with robust infusion of ginger and curry leaves was ready in less than thirty minutes. Ishtoo is rich, creamy and elegant, and is usually served for breakfast along with āpam, idiāppam or dosa. I especially love it with Kerala-style parotta.

*Yield: 4 servings * Prep Time: 10 minutes * Cook Time: 30 minutes*

2 tbsp (28 g) coconut oil

7 to 10 fresh curry leaves (kadi patta)

1 medium red onion, peeled and diced

Small piece fresh ginger (approximately 0.5 oz [10 g]), peeled and diced

3 green chili peppers, or according to taste, slit lengthwise

½ lb (226 g) baby potatoes, quartered, or golden potatoes, diced

1 cup (150 g) frozen mixed vegetables (blend of carrots, green beans and corn)

Salt, to taste

1 tsp ground black pepper (kāli mirch powder)

1 (13.5-oz [400-ml]) can unsweetened full-fat coconut milk, shaken well

In a deep saucepan with a lid, heat the coconut oil over medium heat. Once hot, add the curry leaves and onion. Cook for about 8 minutes, until the onion is soft. Stir in the ginger and chili pepper, and cook for 2 minutes.

Add the potatoes, frozen vegetables, salt and ground black pepper, and stir in the coconut milk.

Fill the empty coconut milk can with a little less than ½ cup (120 ml) water, swirl it around, and add it to the saucepan. The vegetables should be just covered with the liquid.

Bring the mixture to a gentle simmer, covered, over medium heat for 20 minutes, or until the potatoes are fork-tender but still somewhat hold their shape. Uncover, and continue to simmer on low for another 5 to 7 minutes, making sure the vegetables have absorbed all the flavors.

How to Enjoy

Serve hot with rice, rice noodles or any flatbread such as Kerala-style parotta or Malabari parotta. You can find parotta in the frozen aisle of your local Indian store. Check the ingredients list on the pack to make sure it is vegan.

Tips

- *If the stew ends up being too thick because of the variety of the coconut milk, add some hot water to thin it out. Look for a good-quality canned coconut milk, one that has a good aroma, consistency and flavor.*
- *If you do not like the fibrous pieces of ginger but want to retain the gingery flavor in the stew, cut the ginger into larger pieces while adding them so that you can easily remove them before serving.*

Soothing Thayir Sādam

Tempered yogurt rice

In India, yogurt rice goes by many names: curd rice in English, mosaranna in Kannada, and thayir sādam in Tamil. Thayir sādam is rice mixed with unsweetened plain yogurt and a spicy tadkā (tempering). After going vegan, yogurt was one thing that was hard for me to find a substitute for. But I soon found a way to make dairy-free yogurt at home, and today store-bought ones are good quality and available in most stores. The rice for thayir sādam should be well cooked and cooled before mixing in the yogurt. This dish is calming and comforting, and for many Indians a small portion of yogurt rice is how they like to end their everyday meal. It is customizable—some like their yogurt rice plain (without any tempering), others like it with grated carrots or pomegranate arils. My personal preference has always been yogurt rice with tempering of mustard seeds, urad dāl and curry leaves. These add flavor, texture and beauty to the dish. This rich version is one my mom made for potlucks when I was little. It is basic yogurt rice with tempering, but tastes and feels much creamier and decadent because of dairy-free milk and a knob of dairy-free butter.

Yield: 2 servings ✳ *Prep Time: 10 minutes* ✳ *Cook Time: 30 minutes*

2 cups (480 ml) water

½ cup (100 g) uncooked basmati rice, rinsed and drained

1¾ cups (420 ml) plain, unsweetened, dairy-free yogurt

1 tsp salt, or to taste

About ½ cup (120 ml) plain unsweetened dairy-free milk

1 tbsp (14 g) dairy-free butter, softened, optional

1 tsp neutral oil

½ tsp black mustard seeds (rāi)

1 tsp urad dāl (split black lentils)

1 green chili pepper, or according to taste, finely chopped

1 tsp fresh ginger, grated

4 to 5 fresh curry leaves (kadi patta)

¼ tsp hing (asafoetida)

Handful of fresh cilantro, chopped, for serving

In a large saucepan, add the water and drained rice, and stir well to combine. Bring to a boil over medium heat. When the water starts boiling, cover the saucepan, reduce the heat, and cook the rice for 15 to 17 minutes, until all the water is absorbed, stirring occasionally, making sure the rice doesn't burn. Once cooked, turn off the heat, and mix the rice well once again. Set the rice aside to cool for 15 minutes.

Add the yogurt, salt, milk and butter, if using, to the rice, and stir well to combine. You may add more milk or yogurt if you prefer a porridge-like consistency.

Heat the oil in a small tadkā pan or skillet. Add the mustard seeds, and when they begin to pop, gently add the urad dāl. Stir for 30 seconds, and stir in the green chili peppers, ginger and curry leaves. Turn off the heat, and add the hing.

Pour the tadkā over the yogurt rice, add the cilantro, and stir well to combine.

How to Enjoy

- Serve slightly chilled or at room temperature.

- Store any leftovers in the refrigerator for up to a day.

- Serve the yogurt rice as is or with a side stir-fry like Earthy Beet Poriyal (page 121) or Sweet-and-Spicy Shakarkand Bhujiya (page 122) or any achār (see Tip on page 99).

Tip

Alternatively, you may pressure cook the rice for around 4 minutes in an electric pressure cooker and allow the pressure to be released naturally.

Soul-Warming Thukpa

Spicy eastern Indian noodle soup

Start with store-bought noodles and end with serious deliciousness. This warming and nutritious noodle soup is a staple in the northeast region of the subcontinent. I like to make it extra spicy and garlicky, especially on cold winter days.

*Yield: 1 to 2 servings * Prep Time: 15 minutes * Cook Time: 20 minutes*

5.5 oz (150 g) noodles (any variety—buckwheat and rice noodles are some great gluten-free options)

Salt, to taste

3 tbsp (45 ml) neutral oil, divided

1 tsp fresh ginger, grated

2 cloves garlic, minced

3 green onions, finely chopped

⅓ cup (60 g) tomatoes, finely diced

½ tsp ground turmeric (haldi powder)

1 tsp red chili powder (lāl mirch) or cayenne pepper

1 tsp ground cumin (jeera powder)

1 tsp garam masālā (page 165)

Ground black pepper (kāli mirch powder), to taste

¼ tsp Szechuan pepper, ground

5 cups (1.2 L) hot vegetable stock or hot water (see Tips)

1 carrot, julienned

⅓ cup (20 g) cabbage, thinly shredded

1 red bell pepper, finely sliced

1 medium zucchini, peeled and thinly cut into long strips

1 tbsp (15 ml) soy sauce

1 tbsp (15 ml) fresh lime juice, for serving

Handful of fresh cilantro, for serving

Cook the noodles according to package instructions with some salt. Once the noodles become soft, turn off heat. Wait for a minute, then drain. Drizzle 1 tablespoon (15 ml) of the oil on the noodles, toss to coat, and set aside.

To make the soup, preheat a wok over high heat. Add the remaining 2 tablespoons (30 ml) of oil, the ginger and garlic, and cook for 30 seconds. Add the green onions, and continue cooking, stirring continuously. Immediately stir in the tomatoes, and continue to cook for 30 seconds, until soft.

Stir in the ground turmeric, red chili powder, ground cumin, garam masālā, ground black pepper and Szechuan pepper, and continue to cook for a minute, stirring continuously. Gently add the hot vegetable stock to the wok, and bring it to a boil. Add the carrot, cabbage, red bell pepper, zucchini and soy sauce. Cook the vegetables for about 2 minutes. They should still be crunchy.

Check for seasoning, and adjust according to taste.

How to Enjoy

- Spoon the piping-hot soup into bowls; add the noodles, and then top with lime juice and cilantro.

- You can add fried extra-firm tofu to the thukpa as well, if you like. Simply drain the water from a pack of tofu, press it to release excess water, cut tofu into cubes. Heat a nonstick skillet, brush some oil and fry the tofu until the cubes are slightly golden brown on all sides.

Tips

- *If you are using vegetable stock, boil it in a saucepan before you begin. If you are using water, heat it in a kettle or stovetop until boiling.*

- *If you have trouble finding Szechuan peppercorns, try Asian markets or online. To substitute, combine equal quantities of ground black pepper, ground coriander and a pinch of lemon zest.*

Creamy Sarson Ka Saag

Creamy stewed greens

Sarson ka saag, a warming Punjabi dish, traditionally features mustard greens, spinach and bathua greens, stewed with spices and aromatics, and thickened with yellow corn flour. It is creamy and silky, and typically paired with makki ki roti, toasted yellow-corn flatbread. I love the sight of pats of (vegan!) butter melting over both the roti and the saag when served together. Hearty greens can be tough and bitter. Simmering the greens and mashing them while slow-cooking helps tenderize them and give them a comforting silkiness. This process may take some time, but it is truly the best way to cook and eat greens. This recipe is modified to make it quicker and more accessible using easily available ingredients to prepare at home.

*Yield: 4 servings * Prep Time: 25 minutes * Cook Time: 1 hour*

2 large bunches (about 1 lb [454 g] each) fresh mustard greens (sarson), washed thoroughly, stalks discarded, and finely chopped

6 cups (180 g) baby spinach, washed

Salt, to taste

2 green chili peppers, or according to taste

1 bunch fresh cilantro, washed, thick stems discarded

5 cloves garlic, peeled and sliced

4 to 5 tbsp (40 to 50 g) yellow corn flour

1 tbsp (14 g) vegan butter, plus more for serving

1 medium onion, finely chopped

2 small tomatoes, chopped

1 tbsp (6 g) fresh ginger

How to Enjoy

- Serve hot.
- Add a small dollop of vegan butter, if you like, for serving.
- Store any leftovers in the refrigerator. To reheat, add the greens to a saucepan with 2 to 3 tablespoons (30 to 45 ml) of hot water, and bring to a simmer.

In a saucepan, add the mustard greens, baby spinach, salt, green chili peppers, cilantro and garlic, and cook over medium heat, stirring occasionally, until they are tender and mushy, about 45 minutes. During this time, use a potato masher to gently mash the greens, making them tender. Alternatively, you can cook the greens for 30 minutes, and then process them in a blender.

While the greens are cooking, heat about 1½ cups (360 ml) water in a kettle or a pot on the stovetop. After about 45 minutes, and a lot of mashing, add the yellow corn flour to the greens in the saucepan. This gives the greens some body.

Add a scant ¼ cup (60 ml) of hot water to the greens to give them a stew-like consistency. Reduce the heat to low, and continue to simmer the greens while you prepare the tadkā.

In a large skillet over medium heat, heat the vegan butter. Add the onion, season with salt, and sauté until the onion turns light brown. Stir in the tomatoes and ginger, and continue to cook, stirring often, until the tomatoes soften, 5 to 7 minutes. Add the stewed greens to the skillet, mix well to combine, and cook for 5 minutes more. Adjust consistency by adding a few hot spoons of water if the consistency appears thick.

Tips

- *Mustard greens are often seen in the fresh produce section, right by all the other greens.*
- *A dollop of vegan butter to serve is not necessary, but takes the dish up a notch.*
- *Yellow corn flour is found in well-stocked South Asian stores and the baking aisle of most grocery stores. If you are shopping at an Indian grocery store, you can ask for the flour that is used to make makki ki roti.*

Silky Punjabi Kadhi with Pakoda

Sweet and tangy yogurt-based stew

Kadhi is a yogurt-based stew in which plain yogurt is thickened with chickpea flour and finished off with a spice-infused tadkā. It is typically served hot with rice or roti. When I was doing my research for this book, I came across an article that was titled "101 Types of Kadhi From Different Parts of India." It was surprising and not at the same time, considering the diversity of the country. There were many varieties that I had never even heard of. This one that I grew up eating, with pakodas dunked in the stew, is my favorite and reminds me of home—simple, deeply comforting and incredibly complex in its flavor. You may serve the kadhi without the pakoda if you want a quicker meal.

*Yield: 4 servings * Prep Time: 15 minutes * Cook Time: 1 hour*

1½ cups (360 ml) plain, unsweetened, dairy-free yogurt, at room temperature, whisked

½ cup (57 g) besan (chickpea/gram flour), sifted

1 tsp ground turmeric

½ tsp red chili powder (lāl mirch) or cayenne pepper

1 tsp ground coriander

1 tbsp (15 ml) mustard or neutral oil

¼ tsp fenugreek seeds (methi)

½ tsp cumin seeds (jeera)

¼ tsp hing (asafoetida)

1 small red onion, thinly sliced

1 tbsp (6 g) grated fresh ginger

3 cloves of garlic, minced

1 green chili pepper, or according to taste

Salt, to taste

For the Tadkā (Tempering)

1 tbsp (15 ml) neutral oil

1 tsp cumin seeds (jeera)

1 tsp carom seeds (ajwain)

2 whole dried red chilis (any variety)

3 tbsp fresh cilantro, finely chopped, to serve

How to Enjoy

Serve hot over steamed white rice.

Mix the plain unsweetened yogurt and the besan in a large bowl until well combined. Stir in the ground turmeric, red chili powder and the ground coriander along with approximately 6 cups (1.4 L) of water. Whisk until the mixture is smooth and creamy.

In a large saucepan, heat the oil over medium-high and add the fenugreek seeds, cumin seeds and hing, and cook until fragrant, about 30 seconds. Add the sliced onion, ginger, garlic and green chili pepper, and sauté until the onion appears translucent, about 2 minutes. Reduce the heat to low and gently add the prepared yogurt–besan mixture to the saucepan. Increase the heat to medium and bring the mixture to a boil while stirring continuously to prevent the yogurt from curdling or spilling over.

Lower the heat once again and let the mixture simmer until thick and creamy, for about 25 to 30 minutes, making sure to stir every 5 to 7 minutes. Add salt and continue to simmer for another 10 minutes. Turn off the heat.

Make the pakodas (see page 23). Once you are finished frying the pakodas, add them to the kadhi and let them soak for a few minutes while you prepare the tadkā.

For the tadkā, heat the oil over medium heat. Add the cumin seeds, carom seeds and whole dried red chilies in quick succession. After they have sputtered and appear deep in color, about 1 minute, turn off the heat and gently pour the tadkā over the simmering mixture. Sprinkle with chopped cilantro before serving.

Tips

- *You may make bhajiyas/pakodas (page 23) ahead of time, and add them in the kadhi mixture just before serving.*
- *The kadhi should have enough liquid before adding the pakodas. If the consistency is too thick, the pakodas will not be able to soak it up. You can adjust the consistency by adding some hot water.*

Rich Kaju Masala

Roasted cashews in rich and creamy gravy

Four centuries ago, the Portuguese ferried several crops to India. Cashews are one of the ingredients in the Indian pantry that calls back to its Portuguese colonial roots. They are commonly used in several Indian sweet and savory dishes. Kāju masālā, a savory crowd-pleaser, is served in roadside eateries (otherwise known as a "dhaba") in the northern part of the country. The cashews are used in two different ways here—first, they are blended to give the base gravy a creamy texture, and then they are also toasted and added whole.

Yield: 4 servings ✳ *Prep Time: 10 minutes* ✳ *Cook Time: 1 hour*

1¼ cups (175 g) whole unsalted raw cashews, divided

2 small red onions, roughly chopped plus 1 medium red onion, finely chopped

2 tbsp (30 ml) neutral oil

1 tsp cumin seeds (jeera)

3 garlic cloves, minced

1 tbsp fresh ginger, grated

1 green chili pepper, or according to taste, finely chopped

1 medium ripe tomato, finely chopped

Salt, to taste

1 tsp Kashmiri red chili powder

½ tsp ground turmeric (haldi)

2 tsp ground coriander (dhaniya powder)

1 tsp ground cumin (jeera powder)

1 tsp kasuri methi (dry fenugreek leaves)

1 tsp garam masālā (page 165)

½ tsp granulated sugar

Handful of finely chopped fresh cilantro, to serve

2 tbsp (30 ml) unsweetened dairy-free cream, to serve (optional)

In a medium bowl, combine ¼ cup (35 g) of the cashews, the small red onions and enough water to cover them. Bring them to a boil until the cashews have softened and the onions have turned translucent, about 7 to 10 minutes. Drain the water and transfer the onions and cashews into a blender along with ¼ cup (60 ml) of water and process into a smooth paste. Set the paste aside.

In a medium skillet, heat the oil until barely smoking. Add the remaining 1 cup (140 g) of cashews and toast them, stirring often, until golden brown, about 1 minute. Using a slotted spoon, transfer the cashews to a small bowl and set them aside. To the same skillet with the hot oil, add the cumin seeds and cook over medium heat, stirring until fragrant, about 30 seconds. Add the garlic and ginger and cook until the garlic is just beginning to brown, about 45 seconds.

Stir in the medium-sized onion and cook, stirring occasionally, until the onion has turned golden-brown, about 6 to 7 minutes. Add the green chili pepper, tomato, salt, Kashmiri red chili powder, ground turmeric, ground coriander and ground cumin. Cook, stirring until fragrant, for about 1 minute.

Add ½ cup (120 ml) of water. Cover the saucepan and bring to a simmer over medium-high heat, then reduce to medium and simmer, uncovered and stirring occasionally, until the tomatoes have broken down, 3 to 4 minutes.

Stir in the onion-cashew paste, cover and cook, stirring occasionally, until the mixture appears saucy, about 5 minutes. Uncover the skillet and continue to cook until you see some oil on the surface of the sauce. Stir in 1 cup (240 ml) of water and bring the sauce to a gentle simmer. Add the toasted cashews, kasuri methi (crush them between your palms before adding them), garam masālā and granulated sugar and cook over low heat for about 10 minutes. If the mixture appears too thick, add a few spoonfuls of hot water to create a thinner consistency.

Turn off the heat. Sprinkle some fresh cilantro on top. If desired, drizzle with a few spoonfuls of dairy-free cream before serving.

How to Enjoy

Serve with Layered Triangle Parātha (page 66). This is a rich, heavy dish. It is nice to serve a light, refreshing salad as an accompaniment.

Cooking for One

Finding the motivation to cook for oneself can be difficult, especially after a long day at work. Here are some easy, quick and tasty meals that will make the job easy with a little bit of pantry planning. They can be easily doubled when making for more people or stored in the refrigerator if you end up with more servings.

Nutritious Tofu Bhurji

Melt-in-your-mouth scrambled tofu

Protein-packed tofu takes center stage in this creamy, satisfying dish. Inspired by the popular amritsari paneer bhurji, this recipe substitues tofu for the the paneer, which is a dairy cheese. The result, with all the spices and the aromatics, is cruelty-free and tastes just as delicious. The cashew cream makes it rich and luxurious.

Yield: 4 servings ✳ *Prep Time: 15 minutes* ✳ *Cook Time: 45 minutes*

1 tsp neutral oil

1 tsp besan (chickpea/gram flour)

2 cloves garlic, minced

1 tsp fresh ginger, grated

1 medium red onion, finely chopped

2 small ripe tomatoes, finely diced

2 green chili peppers, or according to taste, finely chopped

Salt, to taste

1 tsp ground turmeric (haldi powder)

1 tsp red chili powder (lāl mirch) or cayenne pepper, or according to taste

1 tbsp (6 g) ground coriander (dhaniya powder)

1 (16-oz [454-g]) block firm tofu, drained, pressed and crumbled

Handful of fresh cilantro, washed and finely chopped, divided

2 tbsp (30 ml) cashew cream (page 164) or store-bought, unsweetened, dairy-free cream, plus more for serving, optional

1 tsp kasuri methi (dried fenugreek leaves), crushed

2 tsp (4 g) garam masālā (page 165)

1 tsp chāt masālā (homemade [see page 165] or store-bought)

Heat about 2 cups (480 ml) of water in a kettle or on the stovetop. You will need hot water while cooking, so it is a good idea to have it ready before you begin the cooking process.

In a large skillet over medium-high heat, heat the oil, and toast the besan for 1 minute, stirring constantly so it doesn't burn. Add the garlic, ginger and onion, and sauté for 1 minute. Stir in the tomatoes and green chili peppers. Increase the heat to high, stir well, and cook for about 2 minutes, until the onion and the tomatoes soften.

Reduce the heat to medium, and add the salt, ground turmeric, red chili powder and ground coriander. Stir well, and cook for a minute. Add about ¼ cup (60 ml) of hot water, and continue to cook for another 2 minutes. Add the tofu to the skillet, followed by half of the cilantro, and stir well to combine.

Stir in some more hot water, about ¼ cup (60 ml) or as required to achieve a stew-like consistency. Continue to cook for 2 minutes, stirring occasionally. Add the cashew cream, if using, the kasuri methi and the garam masālā, and stir to combine.

Transfer to a serving platter, and sprinkle with the remaining cilantro and chāt masālā.

How to Enjoy

• Serve with slices of bread (toasted or untoasted) or any kind of flatbread like Layered Triangle Parātha (page 66).

• Any leftovers can be stored in the refrigerator for 1 day. Best when reheated in a skillet over medium heat for 3 to 4 minutes, stirring constantly.

Speedy Sev Tamatar

Sweet and spicy tomato gravy with sev

Sev (gram flour/chickpea flour–fried savory noodles) is something you should always and forever have in your snack cabinet. Other than chāt, or some other kind of street food, I use it often to make this twenty-minute gravy. My mom would make several versions of this for my after-school lunch—sometimes with a pinch of jaggery in the gravy, at other times with a different kind of namkeen (savory crunchy snacks).

Yield: 4 servings ✳ *Prep Time: 10 minutes* ✳ *Cook Time: 20 minutes*

1 tsp neutral oil

1 tsp cumin seeds (jeera)

3 cloves garlic, minced

1 small onion, finely chopped

A few curry leaves (kadi patta), optional (see Tip on page 60)

Pinch of hing (asafoetida)

2 dried bay leaves (tej patta)

4 to 5 medium tomatoes (about 1lb [454 g]), diced (see Tips)

½ tsp ground turmeric (haldi powder)

2 tsp ground coriander (dhaniya powder)

1 tsp Kashmiri red chili powder, or according to taste

Salt, to taste

1 tsp freshly grated ginger

½ tsp granulated sugar

Handful of fresh cilantro, washed and finely chopped

Sev (see Tips)

Heat the oil in a saucepan over medium heat until shimmering. Add the cumin seeds, and cook for about 30 seconds, and then stir in the garlic, onion, curry leaves, if using, and hing. Cook, stirring frequently, until the onion is softened and lightly browned, about 5 minutes.

Add the bay leaves, tomatoes, ground turmeric, ground coriander, Kashmiri red chili powder and salt, and cook for 8 to 10 minutes, stirring occasionally.

Stir in the ginger, sugar and ¾ cup (180 ml) water. Cover and continue to cook for another 5 minutes. Turn off the heat, and stir in the cilantro. Season with some salt, if needed. Top with sev just before serving.

How to Enjoy

- To serve, using your hands, tear a chunk of flatbread or parātha, dip into sev tamatar and eat the whole morsel in one scoop. You can also serve the gravy over rice.

- Any leftovers can be stored in the refrigerator for up to a day. Reheat in the microwave or on the stovetop.

Tips

- *You can also use canned diced tomatoes. Make sure they are not flavored with spices and herbs.*

- *Sev is available in most South Asian stores and in the international food aisle of many large grocery retail chains. Any variety works well here, although I prefer the thicker variety as they hold up well when added to the hot tomato base. The sev should remain slightly crisp and not completely melt into the gravy.*

Savory Masala Toast

A vegan and savory spin on the popular street-style toast

Savory breakfasts are more common in India. It is hard to find anything exclusively sweet served for breakfast (except popular sweet-savory combinations like jalebi-poha, chow-chow bhath, bedmi aloo-nagori halwa, etc.) in many parts of the country. This is a great savory breakfast, work-from-home lunch or even a quick complete meal. I have swapped besan (chickpea/gram flour) for eggs. The tangy and pungent flavor of kāla namak (black salt) makes the batter taste and smell egg-like. The bread soaks up all the intense flavors of the batter and, when toasted, creates this extremely satisfying, crispy, golden-brown exterior.

Yield: 1 serving ✳ *Prep Time: 20 minutes* ✳ *Cook Time: 7 to 10 minutes*

⅓ cup (31 g) besan (chickpea/gram flour)

¼ tsp ground turmeric (haldi powder)

1 tsp ground cumin (jeera powder)

2 green chili peppers, or according to taste, finely chopped

1 tsp fresh ginger, grated

3 cloves garlic, minced

Salt, to taste

¼ tsp garam masālā (homemade [see page 165] or store-bought)

⅛ tsp kāla namak (black salt)

1 small onion, finely chopped (about ⅓ cup [50 g])

1 green onion, finely chopped

1 small firm tomato (about ⅓ cup [60 g]), finely chopped

Handful of fresh cilantro, finely chopped

2 tsp (10 ml) fresh lemon juice

2 to 3 bread slices, any firm variety like sourdough or white country style (see Tips)

Vegan butter or oil, for cooking the toast

1 tsp chāt masālā (homemade [see page 165] or store-bought)

In a wide bowl, whisk together the besan, ground turmeric, ground cumin, chili peppers, ginger, garlic, salt, garam masālā, black salt and about 1 cup (240 ml) water. Stir in the onion, green onion, tomato, cilantro and lemon juice.

Meanwhile, preheat a nonstick (preferably a cast-iron) skillet over medium-low heat.

While the skillet heats, lay a slice of bread into the bowl with the besan mixture, and press it down gently using the back of a spoon, drowning the slice of bread in the batter. Flip the slice of bread, and repeat on the other side, allowing the bread to soak and absorb the batter and some bits of the tomato and onion.

Brush some vegan butter or oil on the skillet, and place the batter-soaked bread in the hot skillet. Cook for about 3 to 5 minutes per side or until golden. Don't be tempted to flip the bread too soon while it is cooking. It only firms up after a fair bit of cooking, which is about 2 to 3 minutes. If you attempt to flip too soon, it might tear.

Transfer to a plate. Sprinkle with some chāt masālā. Repeat with the remaining batter and bread slices.

How to Enjoy
Serve immediately while still hot with ketchup or mint-cilantro chutney (page 164).

Tips
- *Fresh bread is not recommended for this recipe; I would suggest using 1-day old bread. The slice of bread needs to be able to withstand a good soaking and pan-frying without falling apart. Use thick slices and a slightly dense variety.*
- *Make sure the skillet is medium-hot and sizzles when you place the batter-soaked slice of bread in it. If the skillet is not hot, the bread will stick to the skillet.*

Zingy Fruit Chat

Fresh seasonal fruits combined with ground robust spices and lemon juice

Fruity, savory and refreshing, that's fruit chāt. Popular in the streets of many Indian towns and cities, this dish is a savory assortment of seasonal fruits. In India, tropical fruits are always found in abundance. In this mixed fruit chāt, chunks of fruits are dusted with chāt masālā (which makes this chatpata, meaning a combination of spicy, sour, tangy), nuts and fresh mint. This recipe is the epitome of customizable—you may add more or less of any fruit depending on what is available or to suit your preference.

*Yield: 1 serving * Prep Time: 10 minutes*

1 guava, thinly sliced

1 small papaya, peeled and cut into thin, small wedges

Pomegranate arils, to taste

1 apple, diced

Handful of grapes

Small oranges, segmented

Fresh mint, stems discarded and leaves finely chopped

1 tsp fresh lemon juice

Chāt masālā (homemade [see page 165] or store-bought)

½ tsp ground cumin (jeera powder)

Unsalted toasted nuts, such as slivered almonds, optional

In a large bowl, combine the guava, papaya, pomegranate, apple, grapes and oranges. Add the mint, lemon juice, chāt masālā and ground cumin. Allow the fruit to rest for about 10 minutes, to let the flavors infuse, and then serve topped with toasted nuts, if using.

How to Enjoy
Serve within 1 hour of preparation.

Tip

Any seasonal fruit works here. Just make sure that the fruit you are using is ripe but still firm and holding shape. Some other fruits that I like to add are pineapple, golden kiwi and blueberries.

Spicy Jhal Muri

Spiced puffed rice seasoned with raw mustard oil

Growing up, my family and I would travel to India to visit our close relatives. After landing in Bombay, which is in the west of India, we would go on a long train journey to the eastern part of the country to visit my maternal grandparents. Once the train got closer to the eastern cities, at every train station, I would see a jhāl muri vendor. Jhāl means "spicy" and muri is puffed rice. The most memorable jhāl muri are those served on trains during long journeys, by traveling vendors who board the train with their modest jhāl muri setup hanging from their neck, sort of like a portable table with tiny pockets to hold the various components of this snack. But hygiene was a priority in my family (I blame our poor immune system for this), and I never ate the best kind of jhāl muri, the street stalls or train station kind. The vendor would scoop the muri into a dechki (stainless steel mixing container), stir in all the other ingredients like a chef doing a wok-toss and serve them beautifully in a thonga (small paper bag). The secret ingredient here is oil from a jar of achār (mango pickle), which is infused with spicy and warming flavors.

Yield: 2 to 4 servings ✳ *Prep Time: 15 minutes* ✳ *Assembly Time: 10 minutes*

1 tbsp (6 g) cumin seeds (jeera)

1 tbsp (6 g) fennel seeds (saunf)

1 tsp coriander seeds (dhaniya)

1 green cardamom pod (elaichi)

1 cup (18 g) puffed rice (muri)

¼ tsp kāla namak (black salt)

1 small red onion, finely chopped

1 small tomato, seeds and pulp removed, finely diced

1 small cucumber, seeds removed, finely diced

2 green chili peppers, or according to taste, crushed

1 small potato (about ¼ cup [20 g]) boiled, cooled and diced

Oil from a jar of mango pickles (mango achār) (see Tips)

1 tbsp (15 ml) mustard oil

1 tsp fresh lemon juice

Heat a small skillet over medium heat. Add the cumin seeds, fennel seeds, coriander seeds and the green cardamom pod to the skillet, and toast them until fragrant, 3 to 4 minutes, stirring continuously. Turn off the heat, and transfer the spices to a plate.

While the spices are cooling, toast the puffed rice for a couple of minutes in the same skillet over medium heat, stirring continuously. You may also microwave it for 30 seconds.

Grind the roasted spices (bhaja masālā) using a spice grinder or mortar and pestle.

To a large, wide mixing bowl, add the toasted puffed rice, the bhaja masālā, the black salt, onion, tomato, cucumber, green chili peppers and potato.

Add the oil from the mango pickles, the mustard oil and fresh lemon juice. Mix everything thoroughly. Check for seasoning and adjust accordingly, if needed.

How to Enjoy

• Serve immediately in a paper cone or a bowl.

• Store any leftover puffed rice in an airtight container.

Tips

• You will find puffed rice (muri) in South Asian stores—the most common name on the pack will be kurmura, murmura, mamra or puffed rice.

• Achār (pickle) is a popular condiment in Indian cuisine. It adds a tangy, salty heat when paired with rice and rotis.

Satisfying Sweet Corn Soup

Comforting corn and vegetable soup

When you have a busy life (who doesn't?), cooking is a balance between speed and flavor, and I would rather not compromise on flavor. This silky smooth soup with the rich flavor from the corn and chunky bits of vegetables is a quick, easy, home-style version of the Indo-Chinese favorite. A big bowl will leave you satisfied for hours!

Yield: 2 servings ✳ *Prep Time: 15 minutes* ✳ *Cook Time: 15 to 20 minutes*

1 cup (150 g) sweet corn, fresh or frozen, divided (see Tip)

1 tbsp (15 ml) neutral oil

1 green chili pepper, or according to taste, chopped

10 fresh green beans, ends trimmed and finely chopped

1 small carrot, peeled and finely diced

½ cup (70 g) frozen green peas

1 tsp fresh ginger, grated

1 tbsp (15 g) granulated sugar

Salt, to taste

½ tsp ground white pepper

¼ tsp ground black pepper (kāli mirch powder)

1 tbsp (9 g) cornstarch

2 tbsp (30 ml) water

2 green onions, finely chopped, for serving

Heat about 4 cups (960 ml) of water in the kettle or on the stovetop. Blend together ½ cup (75 g) of the corn and a little less than ½ cup (120 ml) of hot water until the texture is slightly grainy but no big chunks of corn remain.

To a large saucepan over medium heat, add the oil, and heat it for a minute. Add the green chili pepper, green beans, carrot, green peas and the remaining ½ cup (75 g) of corn, and sauté for 10 minutes, stirring occasionally.

Stir in the blended sweet corn and about 2 cups (480 ml) water, and bring the mixture to a boil, skimming off any foam that you see on the surface.

Add the ginger, sugar, salt, white pepper and black pepper, and continue to simmer.

In a small bowl, combine the cornstarch and water, stirring to combine. Add the cornstarch slurry to the saucepan, reduce the heat to low, and simmer for 5 minutes. Turn off the heat, taste and adjust seasonings if needed.

How to Enjoy

- Serve piping-hot with green onions and additional black pepper.
- Store any leftovers in the refrigerator in an airtight container. The soup tastes best when fresh. Reheating the soup on the stovetop is the best option. The soup thickens after refrigeration. In that case, add hot water and adjust seasoning.

Tip

Use fresh corn when it is in season. If you are using frozen corn, remember to thaw it for at least 15 minutes before using.

Ideal for Dabba: Lunch Box Favorites

These dishes have always been my favorite to carry to school, and it is heartwarming to see how my daughter gets excited about the very same dishes. All the recipes in this chapter can be easily transported and taste delicious even a few hours after they have been prepared. Sabudana khichdi (page 112) needs a bit of planning in advance because of the soaking step involved, but the rest of the dishes can be made quickly and easily without any advance preparation.

Fresh Carrot Kosambari

Grated carrot salad with a spicy tempering

The only vegetable I would eat as a kid was potato. I had mentally catalogued every other vegetable as something I would never try. Until one day, when my mom rolled up a roti with this carrot salad for my after-school snack. It was refreshing and delicious, and it quickly became a lunch box favorite! It is super quick to whip up and makes a wonderfully simple lunch box addition. A typical South Indian dish, it ticks off all the sweet, salty and spicy boxes. There's so much textural joy here, too, with the crunch of the lentils and nuts to finish things off.

*Yield: 4 servings * Prep Time: 15 minutes (plus soaking time) * Cook Time: 10 minutes*

2 tbsp (25 g) moong dāl (split moong/mung beans), rinsed and drained

2 cups (220 g) carrots, peeled and grated (see Tips)

1 tbsp (15 ml) neutral oil

2 tsp (6 g) black mustard seeds (rāi)

1 tsp urad dāl (split white lentils)

1 tbsp (10 g) chana dāl (dalia or roasted split chickpeas)

2 green chili peppers, or according to taste, cut in half lengthwise

Salt, to taste

½ tsp ground turmeric (haldi powder)

Juice of 1 medium lemon, or to taste

½ cup (50 g) toasted unsalted pistachios or peanuts, coarsely chopped

½ bunch fresh cilantro, finely chopped

In a small bowl, soak the moong dāl in water for about an hour. After that, drain the moong dāl into a colander and set aside until ready to use. Squeeze out any excess moisture from the grated carrots, and put them into a large bowl.

Heat the oil in a skillet over medium-high heat until shimmering. Add the black mustard seeds and cook until they begin to splutter, about 30 seconds. Add the urad dāl and chana dāl, and cook, stirring continuously, until they turn slightly brown, about 45 seconds. Add the chili peppers, and stir quickly to prevent it from burning.

Stir in the grated carrots, moong dāl, salt and ground turmeric, and turn off the heat. Stir well to combine. Stir in the lemon juice, pistachios and cilantro. Taste and season with more salt or lemon juice, if needed.

How to Enjoy

- Serve at room temperature as a large salad, side salad, wrapped inside flatbreads for lunch box, etc.
- Store any leftovers in the refrigerator for a day.

Tips

- *Grated cabbage or shaved fennel also works well here in place of carrots.*
- *You can also buy pre-grated carrots in the fresh produce aisle.*

Umami Hakka Noodles

Easy street-style Indo-Chinese noodles

Kolkata (formerly Calcutta) is the birthplace of Indo-Chinese food, which traces back to the Hakka Chinese traders who settled here in the late 1700s. Kolkata was the capital of British India at that time. Don't worry, I am not going to take you deep into the history, but I want to introduce you to the cuisine, which is hugely popular all over India. Back then, Chinese immigrants started cooking their food using the ingredients that were available to them locally and started opening restaurants in the city, as their street food was becoming a favorite of the locals. The best way to describe Indo-Chinese food would be Chinese food adapted to Indian tastes. In India, it is referred to as simply "Chinese food." It is a uniquely South Asian phenomenon, and when a South Asian says, "Let's go eat Chinese food," they mean dishes like gobi manchurian, hakka noodles, manchow soup, etc., not the Chinese food from China.

There are distinct flavors in Indo-Chinese cooking, like the Schezwan sauce (my favorite), which uses dry red chilies, and the Manchurian sauce, which is a classic, spicy, soy-based sauce with Indian aromatics like ginger, garlic and green chili peppers. It is fascinating to see how Indo-Chinese food has evolved over the years. These days, well-stocked grocery stores in Indian cities and South Asian grocery stores outside India carry instant noodles for Hakka-style noodles, manchow soup packets, premade sauces, etc. Another fascinating concept that was born out of the Indo-Chinese cuisine is fusion dishes—like Chinese bhel, chili-idli or Chinese pakoda, to name a few.

Yield: 6 to 8 servings ✳ *Prep Time: 25 to 30 minutes* ✳ *Cook Time: 10 minutes*

Salt, to taste

1 tsp plus 4 tbsp (70 ml) neutral oil, divided

1 large pack of noodles (see Tips)

3 cloves garlic, minced

1 large red onion, thinly sliced and layers separated

5 green onions, green and white parts chopped, plus 3 green onions for serving

1 large carrot, peeled and cut into long, thin strips

2 medium green bell peppers, cut into long, thin strips

2 cups (140 g) or 1 small head cabbage, shredded or cut into long, thin strips

1 tsp granulated sugar

Bring a large saucepan or Dutch oven of water to a rolling boil. Salt the water, add 1 teaspoon of the oil, and gently drop the noodles into the water. Cook the noodles according to package instructions, until the strands start to separate from each other, about 1 minute.

Turn off the heat, and cover the saucepan or Dutch oven with a lid. Let it rest for 2 minutes. Drain the noodles into a colander, and rinse the noodles with water for 10 seconds. Set the noodles aside.

Heat a large wok or skillet over medium-high heat. Once the wok appears smoky, add the remaining 4 tablespoons (60 ml) of the oil, swirling the wok around to coat the surface with oil evenly.

Add the garlic, stir for 10 seconds, then increase the heat to high. Add the onions, and cook, stirring continuously, for 10 seconds. Stir in the carrot, bell peppers, cabbage and sugar in quick succession, and cook for 30 seconds. The vegetables should not cook for too long and should retain their crunch.

(continued)

Umami Hakka Noodles (continued)

1 tsp ground black pepper

1 tsp ground white pepper

2 tbsp (30 ml) light soy sauce

1 tsp chili oil, optional

1 tsp white vinegar

Add the cooked noodles to the hot wok or skillet, and season with salt. Add the ground black pepper, ground white pepper, soy sauce, chili oil, if using, and white vinegar, and continue to stir for about 1 minute, until the noodle strands are heated well and coated with the sauce.

Turn off the heat, top with chopped green onions, and serve hot.

How to Enjoy
- Serve with a fork or chopsticks.
- If you are packing this for a lunch box, you may slightly undercook the noodles and the veggies and pack the dish in a thermos.

Tips

- *You can find instant (dried) Hakka-style noodles in most South Asian grocery stores. They are called instant noodles as they are partially cooked, and when you make these noodles, you add them to hot boiling water and rest them just enough to rehydrate them. If you are unable to find Hakka-style noodles, you may use any other kind as well. Be sure to follow the package instructions for cooking the noodles to al dente.*

- *It is important to chop/julienne the vegetables into long, thin strips so when they are briefly cooked, they retain the right crunchy texture.*

- *Make sure you have all the ingredients set up right next to the wok while cooking, because you are cooking the noodles and the vegetables over high heat, and they should not be any delay while adding the ingredients.*

Light Lemon Sevai with Coconut Chutney

Rice noodles, cooked and tossed with fresh lemon juice and tempering

These savory rice noodles of South India fall under the "tiffin" category, a light meal. Traditionally they are prepared using a sevai nazhi, which is a large press to extrude the rice noodle dough. It is labor-intensive for the ones making it, but a rewarding experience for the ones eating and watching it being made. It is meditative to watch how a ball of soft rice dough gets transformed into delicate strings. These days, instant rice sevai packs are easily available, just like packaged noodles. You add them to hot boiling water, and they are ready, acting as a blank canvas for your favorite seasonings and tadkā. This is my favorite way to season and flavor instant sevai noodles. I love the slightly citrusy flavor from the lemon juice, with bursts of texture from the tadkā and the nuts, and the delightful aroma of the curry leaves.

Yield: 6 to 8 servings ✶ *Prep Time: 10 minutes* ✶ *Cook Time: 15 minutes*

1 (17.5-oz [500-g]) package instant sevai (see Tips)

2 tbsp (30 ml) neutral oil

1 tbsp (11 g) black mustard seeds (rāi)

1 tsp urad dāl (split white lentils)

2 green chili peppers, or according to taste, finely chopped

4 curry leaves (kadi patta) (optional but highly recommended, see Tips)

Pinch of hing (asafoetida)

1 tsp ground turmeric (haldi powder)

Handful of unsalted cashews and/or peanuts

Fresh lemon juice from ½ lemon, or as needed

Bring a large Dutch oven filled halfway with water to a boil. When the water begins to boil vigorously, turn off the heat, drop the instant sevai into it, and cover the pot for 3 to 4 minutes, allowing the noodles to turn soft and tender. Drain the sevai into a colander and set aside.

Heat the oil in a tadkā pan or skillet over medium heat, and add the mustard seeds. When they begin to pop, add the urad dāl and green chili peppers, and cook for 30 seconds. Turn off the heat. Gently add the curry leaves, hing, and the ground turmeric. Add the cashews to the pan, and toast in the residual heat, stirring often.

Transfer the sevai from the colander to the Dutch oven, and pour the tempering on the sevai. Stir well to combine using a fork. Add the lemon juice, stir again, taste and adjust seasoning, if needed.

(continued)

Light Lemon Sevai with Coconut Chutney *(continued)*

For the Coconut Chutney

1 cup (80 g) fresh or frozen (thawed) unsweetened coconut

3 green chili peppers, or according to taste

1 tbsp (12 g) chana dāl (dalia or roasted split chickpeas)

Salt, to taste

1 tsp neutral oil

1 tsp black mustard seeds (rāi)

1 tsp urad dāl (split white lentils)

1 whole dried red chili

3 fresh curry leaves (kadi patta) (see Tips)

For the coconut chutney, in a blender, combine the coconut, green chili peppers, chana dāl, ¾ cup (180 ml) hot water and salt.

Heat a tadkā pan over medium-high heat, then add the oil and black mustard seeds. Once the seeds begin to pop, add the urad dāl and dried red chili. Turn off the heat, carefully add the curry leaves to the tadka pan, then add the tadkā to the coconut chutney. Adjust seasoning and consistency by adding more hot water, if needed. You can make it thick and chunky or soupy.

How to Enjoy

Pair the Light Lemon Sevai with Coconut Chutney or Minty Rasam (page 73). If you are packing the sevai for a lunch box, a cup of unsweetened dairy-free yogurt is good option for an accompaniment.

Tips

- *You can find sevai in most South Asian grocery stores. The name on the pack is usually instant rice sevai, or rice vermicelli. Most commonly available brands of instant sevai are MTR or 777. Check the package for instructions on how to prepare the basic sevai. Some brands may have different suggestions.*

- *Fresh curry leaves will be available in well-stocked South Asian stores. There is no substitute.*

Fulfilling Sabudana Khichdi

Tapioca pearl pilaf with peanuts and potatoes

Anyone who has had sabudana khichdi loves it, because it has the perfect balance of texture and flavor. Sabudana or sago is an edible starch extracted from the spongy center of the tapioca plant. When I made it for my daughter the first time, she was little, and she exclaimed, "This is the best thing I have ever eaten!" But let's just say that is something she says often regarding meals that I make.

*Yield: 2 servings * Prep Time: 15 minutes, plus soaking time * Cook Time: 20 minutes*

1½ cups (270 g) sabudana (sago or tapioca pearls)

3 tbsp (45 ml) neutral oil

2 tsp (3 g) cumin seeds (jeera)

3 to 4 green chili peppers, or according to taste, finely chopped

4 to 5 curry leaves (kadi patta) (optional but highly recommended, see Tip on page 111)

1 medium potato, peeled and diced into 2-inch (5-cm) cubes

¾ cup (100 g) roasted unsalted peanuts, coarsely ground

Salt, to taste

1 tsp granulated sugar

½ tsp fresh lemon juice

Handful of fresh cilantro, finely chopped

Pomegranate arils, for serving, optional

Rinse the tapioca pearls in a colander under running water two to three times, and drain out all the water. In a large bowl, soak the drained tapioca pearls in water for 4 to 6 hours (up to overnight) or until all the water is absorbed. The pearls should be moist but not wet. There should be no excess water after the soaking process. You can test if the tapioca pearls are soaked well by pressing a few pearls between your fingers. If they are perfectly soaked, they will be soft and easily get pressed. Use a 1:1 ratio of tapioca pearls and water.

Once you are set to make the sabudana khichdi, gently fluff the soaked tapioca pearls with a spoon to make sure the pearls have absorbed the water and that there is no remaining water in the bowl.

Heat the oil in a wide skillet over medium heat, and add the cumin seeds. Once the seeds start to sizzle, carefully add the green chili peppers, curry leaves, if using, and the potatoes. Reduce the heat to low, and give the ingredients a quick stir. Cover and cook until the potatoes are fork-tender, 7 to 10 minutes. It is important to cook at the lowest heat at this stage to make sure the chili peppers and potatoes don't burn.

Uncover the skillet, and add the soaked tapioca pearls, the peanuts, salt and sugar, and mix well, making sure everything is well combined. The ground peanuts will absorb any remaining moisture in the tapioca pearls making them soft, light and fluffy.

Cover the skillet and cook for about 7 to 10 minutes, stirring every 4 minutes, until the tapioca pearls are soft, not clumped together, and translucent. Turn off the heat, and stir in the lemon juice and cilantro.

Serve with pomegranate arils, if using.

How to Enjoy

- This is best served hot, however you may refrigerate any leftovers for up to a day. Serve alongside a bowl of dairy-free plain yogurt.
- You can reheat by microwaving the khichdi in 30-second intervals. If it feels too dry because of refrigeration, sprinkle a few drops of water, cover, and reheat.

Nourishing Kāla Chana Chāt

Nutrient-packed black chickpea salad

This protein-packed salad is made with black chickpeas and found commonly in the streets of northern India. I love having this for a brunch because it is filling and satisfying. It needs a little bit of planning in advance, because the black chickpeas need to be soaked before they can be cooked. After that, it is just assembling the different ingredients together just like you would make any salad.

Yield: 1 serving ✳ *Prep Time: 20 minutes, plus soaking time* ✳ *Cook Time: 20 minutes*

¾ cup (150 g) kāla chana (black chickpeas)

Salt, to taste

2 tbsp (30 ml) neutral oil

½ tsp hing (asafoetida)

1 black cardamom pod (badi elaichi)

4 whole cloves (lavang)

6 black peppercorns (kāli mirch)

1 tbsp (6 g) fresh ginger, grated

½ tsp red chili powder (lāl mirch) or cayenne pepper, or according to taste

1 tsp ground turmeric (haldi powder)

1 tbsp (6 g) ground coriander (dhaniya powder)

¾ tsp kasuri methi (dry fenugreek leaves)

1 medium potato, boiled and diced

1 small onion, finely chopped

1 small tomato, diced

½ tsp kāla namak (black salt)

½ tsp ground cumin (jeera powder)

1 tsp chāt masālā (homemade [see page 165] or store-bought)

Fresh lemon juice, to taste

Handful of fresh cilantro, finely chopped

Pomegranate arils, optional

Soak the dry kāla chana in warm water for at least 6 hours.

Drain the soaked the kāla chana in a colander, and cook them with some salt in a pressure cooker until soft, about 15 minutes. The kāla chana should be cooked enough to break when pressed between your fingers but still retain their shape. Reserve the cooking water, and set aside.

In a large skillet, heat the oil over medium heat. Add the hing, whole cardamom, whole cloves, black peppercorns and ginger, and sauté for 1 minute, stirring continuously. Stir in the red chili powder, ground turmeric, ground coriander and kasuri methi, and continue to stir for a minute.

Add the cooked kāla chana, along with 1 cup (240 ml) of the cooking water, season with salt, and cook, stirring often, until the water has evaporated, 7 to 10 minutes. Turn off the heat, and set the chickpeas to cool. This process helps the kāla chana absorb the flavors from the spices.

In a large serving bowl, add the kāla chana, potato, onion, tomato, black salt, ground cumin, chāt masālā, lemon juice and cilantro, and stir until well combined.

Taste and adjust seasoning, if needed. Stir in the pomegranate arils and serve immediately.

How to Enjoy
Serve as a side salad, main salad or wrapped inside a flatbread.

Tips
- *Kāla chana can be found in well-stocked South Asian grocery stores. You can find them in the lentils and pulses section.*
- *Feel free to add more or less of any ingredient to suit your palate.*

Protein-Packed Mugachi Usal

Sprouted stir-fried mung beans

Sprouts are common in Indian cuisine. They are used in sabzis, soups and salads. This stir-fry is not just healthy, it is filling and flavorful. Usal, typically a stir-fry made of pulses and lentils and commonly made in the Konkan region of India, is a wonderful way to use the sprouted lentils, and I love using moong dāl most of the time. There are many delicious versions of usal and this one is my go-to.

Yield: 4 servings ✻ *Prep Time: 20 minutes, plus sprouting time* ✻ *Cook Time: 30 minutes*

1½ cups (300 g) whole moong dāl (whole moong/mung beans)

1 tbsp (15 ml) neutral oil

1 tsp black mustard seeds (rāi)

1 tbsp (6 g) cumin seeds (jeera)

3 to 4 fresh curry leaves (kadi patta), optional

Pinch of hing (asafoetida)

1 large onion, finely chopped

2 green chili peppers, or according to taste, crushed

3 cloves garlic, minced

1 tbsp (6 g) fresh ginger, grated

Handful of fresh cilantro, finely chopped

½ tbsp (4 g) ground turmeric (haldi powder)

1 tsp ground fennel (saunf powder)

1 medium tomato, diced into small pieces

1 tbsp (6 g) ground coriander (dhaniya powder)

1 tsp red chili powder (lāl mirch) or cayenne pepper, or according to taste

1 tbsp (6 g) garam masālā (homemade [see page 165] or store-bought)

Salt, to taste

Fresh lemon juice

Toasted unsalted peanuts, coarsely chopped, optional

To sprout the moong dāl, rinse and soak them in a large pot with warm water. Cover and let them rest for at least 8 hours in a warm place in your kitchen. Make sure there is enough water to cover the surface of the moong completely, about 3 cups (720 ml) of water.

After the soak time, drain the water from the moong dāl using a colander. Rinse them, spread a clean cheesecloth over a strainer, and transfer the soaked moong dāl on the cloth. Gather the ends of the cloth, and secure them by leaving at least 2-inch (5-cm) gap. Place the cloth pouch over the strainer, and leave it in a dark spot on the kitchen counter or inside an oven that is turned off for 9 to 10 hours. You will notice the seeds have begun to sprout.

To make the mugachi usal, heat a large skillet over medium heat. Add the oil. Add the black mustard seeds, and once they begin to pop, about 30 seconds, add the cumin seeds. Gently add the curry leaves, hing and onion, and sauté, stirring continuously, until the onion begins to brown, 5 to 7 minutes.

Add the green chili peppers, garlic, ginger and cilantro, and sauté for 2 minutes, stirring often. Stir in ground turmeric, ground fennel, tomato, ground coriander, red chili powder and garam masālā, and continue to sauté for 2 minutes, stirring often. Season with salt, and add the sprouted mung beans. Mix well until combined.

Add about a cup of water, cover, and cook over medium-low heat until the mung beans absorb all the water, about 10 minutes. Turn off the heat, and stir in the fresh lemon juice and peanuts, if using.

How to Enjoy

- Serve hot or at room temperature with any flatbread or Layered Triangle Parātha (page 66) or as a salad.

- Sprouted beans can be stored in the refrigerator in an airtight container for 2 to 3 days.

Hidden One-Pot Gems

Dishes in this chapter require only one pot. Prepping and cleaning will be a breeze. From various rice dishes to a delicious tofu dish, this chapter has everyone covered. Each recipe has its own unique flair. Vibrant vegetables and grains liven up these easy dishes with bright colors, fresh flavors and powerful nutrients—all in one pot.

Earthy Beet Poriyal

Easy stir-fried beets with chickpeas and coconut

Poriyal is a classic South Indian side dish usually made with a single vegetable, giving the vegetable a star status. Most popular vegetables used to make poriyal are green beans, carrots and cabbage. Various names exist for seemingly identical dishes across India, because India is vast and the population is varied. Depending on where in South India it comes from, this classic stir-fry is known variously as poriyal (in Tamil Nadu), thoran (in Kerala) or palya (in Karnataka). This version with chickpeas is one of my dad's signature dishes. It adds a nice textural interest and, of course, protein.

Yield: 4 servings as a side dish ✳ *Prep Time: 15 minutes* ✳ *Cook Time: 35 to 40 minutes*

1 tsp neutral or coconut oil

2 tsp (6 g) black mustard seeds (rāi)

2 tsp (8 g) chana dāl (dalia or roasted split chickpeas)

2 tsp (10 g) white urad dāl

4 fresh curry leaves (kadi patta), optional (see Tip on page 111)

Thai chili pepper, or chili pepper of choice, split in half lengthwise

1 medium onion, finely chopped

1 tsp ground turmeric (haldi powder)

4 medium beets, approximately 4½ cups (610 g), washed, peeled and diced into small pieces

Salt, to taste

1 (15.5-oz [439-g]) can chickpeas, rinsed and drained

¼ cup (20 g) unsweetened grated coconut (fresh or frozen)

In a large skillet with a lid, heat the oil over medium-high heat until shimmering. Add the black mustard seeds. Once they begin to pop, after about a minute, reduce the heat to low. Add the chana dāl, urad dāl and curry leaves, and cook, stirring frequently, until fragrant, about 15 seconds. Add the chili pepper, and continue to cook, stirring, about 7 seconds.

Add the onion and ground turmeric, and continue to cook, stirring constantly, until slightly softened, about 2 minutes.

Add the beets, season with salt, and sprinkle with 2 tablespoons (30 ml) of water. Cover and cook, stirring occasionally, until the beets are fully cooked, about 15 minutes. Uncover and cook until any remaining liquid has evaporated.

Stir in the chickpeas, and cook for 7 to 10 minutes, stirring occasionally. Sprinkle the coconut over the beets and chickpeas, stir until thoroughly combined, and remove from the heat. Season to taste with salt. Serve warm or at room temperature.

How to Enjoy

- To make a meal of it, serve as a side dish, warm or at room temperature with Soothing Thayir Sādam (page 78) or with Minty Rasam (page 73) and white rice.
- The poriyal can be reheated in the microwave or on the stovetop.

Tips

- *You must use fresh grated coconut or fresh grated coconut that has been frozen, and not desiccated. If you are using the frozen variety, make sure you thaw a small portion before you start the cooking process. For convenience, try to find the frozen variety, sold in packets that are in the frozen section of well-stocked South Asian grocery stores.*
- *Beets contain color pigments that can stain hands, clothes and chopping surfaces. If you get beet juice on yourself, wash it as quickly as possible to keep the stains from setting in.*

Sweet and Spicy Shakarkand Bhujiya

Stir-fried crispy sweet potatoes with mild spices

This is my grandma's recipe re-imagined. Aloo (potato) bhujiya and a few Layered Triangle Parāthas (page 66) would be her go-to lunch box meal that she often packed for me (during the short time I lived with her). She would make it in her iron kadhai, which gave the potatoes a crispy exterior. I make it with sweet potatoes and garlic often, which she did not, but my daughter loves how the flavors work well together. This dish is so simple, it's unbelievable.

Yield: 2 servings as a side dish ✳ Prep Time: 10 minutes ✳ Cook Time: 20 minutes

1 large sweet potato

2 tbsp (30 ml) neutral oil or mustard oil

½ tsp cumin seeds (jeera)

2 cloves garlic, minced

1 tsp red chili powder (lāl mirch) or cayenne pepper, or according to taste

¼ tsp ground turmeric (haldi powder)

1 tbsp (6 g) ground coriander

Salt, to taste

Fresh cilantro, washed and finely chopped

1 tsp fresh lemon juice

Peel the sweet potato, wash it, and cut it into thick rounds. Cut each round lengthwise into ½-inch- (1-cm-) wide strips.

In a nonstick skillet with a lid, heat the oil over medium-high heat until just smoking. Add the cumin seeds. Cook the cumin seeds until they begin to sizzle, 7 to 10 seconds. Reduce the heat to medium, add the garlic, and cook, stirring, for 10 seconds. Stir in the sweet potato, followed by the red chili powder, ground turmeric and ground coriander. Sprinkle a few drops of water, give it a stir, cover, and cook on medium heat for about 10 minutes, stirring occasionally and adjusting the heat as necessary. Don't stir too often, as you want the sweet potatoes to have reasonably crisp and brown edges.

After about 10 minutes, remove the lid, add salt, and check the sweet potato for doneness. You can use a fork to test to see if they are tender enough. Your fork should easily slide through the sweet potato rounds when they're fully cooked. If they still appear firm, cover and continue to cook for another 5 to 7 minutes, and check for doneness once again.

Once they are cooked, turn off the heat, and stir in the cilantro and lemon juice.

How to Enjoy

- Serve hot or at room temperature.

- Store any leftover in the refrigerator for up to a day and reheat in the microwave or on the stovetop.

- For a full meal, serve Sweet-and-Spicy Shakarkand Bhujiya (page 122) with Mouthwatering Pānch Phoran Dāl (page 46) or on the side with Layered Triangle Parātha (page 66).

Tip

You can make potato, yam, or pretty much any root vegetable stir-fry with this recipe, but the cooking time will vary.

Tangy Tomato Rice

Basmati rice cooked in a spicy, tangy tomato sauce

This is one of the dishes that never existed in our household, and suddenly one day, it made a special appearance for lunch when I got back home from school. It quickly became a weekly staple and my brother, Chirag's, favorite dish. I love adding a lot of garlic and fresh green chilies, and the key to taking this tomato rice to the next level is to use fresh tomatoes instead of canned ones. It really makes a difference. When I lived in Belgium, I would use up leftover rice by adding spices to store-bought passata and mixing everything together to make a quick variation of tomato rice. It tasted fantastic at the time, but now I would never go back to passata. Fresh tomatoes make a world of difference.

Yield: 4 servings ✳ Prep Time: 15 minutes ✳ Cook Time: 45 to 50 minutes (including rice soaking time)

1½ cups (300 g) basmati rice

3 tbsp (45 ml) neutral oil

1 tsp black mustard seeds (rāi)

2-inch (5-cm) cinnamon stick (dālchini)

2 dried bay leaves (tej patta)

3 green chili peppers, or according to taste, finely chopped

6 cloves garlic, minced

2-inch (5-cm) piece fresh ginger, grated

1 large red onion, finely chopped

5 medium tomatoes, diced

2 tsp (12 g) salt, or to taste

1 tsp ground turmeric (haldi powder)

1 tbsp (6 g) ground coriander (dhaniya powder)

Handful of chopped fresh cilantro, plus more for serving

Tip
I strongly recommend using fresh ripe tomatoes, fresh ginger and fresh garlic for this dish. If you prefer using canned diced tomatoes, adjust the water while cooking, as the canned variety will have a lot of juice.

Wash the rice in a bowl with your fingers. Once the water turns cloudy, drain it, and repeat until the water appears clear. Soak the rice in a bowl with some cold water for about 15 minutes.

In a large saucepan over medium-high heat, heat the oil. Add the black mustard seeds, and cook for 30 seconds until they begin to pop. Add the cinnamon stick, bay leaves, chili peppers, garlic and ginger, stirring continuously. Add the onion and cook, stirring frequently, until light brown, 5 to 7 minutes.

Stir in the tomatoes with their juices, the salt, ground turmeric, ground coriander and cilantro, and cook until the tomatoes soften, 5 to 7 minutes.

Drain the rice that has been soaking, and add it to the saucepan. Mix well to coat the rice grains with the sauce.

Add 2 cups (480 ml) of water, and stir well to combine. Bring it to a gentle simmer over medium heat for about 5 minutes.

Give the rice a quick stir, reduce the heat to low, and cover the saucepan. Let the rice cook for 8 to 10 minutes or until all the water is absorbed. Do not be tempted to uncover the lid too many times during this stage. The steam will help cook the rice completely without letting it burn or get overcooked.

Turn off the heat. Remove the lid, and gently fluff the rice using a fork. Discard the cinnamon stick and bay leaf, and sprinkle with fresh cilantro before serving.

How to Enjoy
- Serve hot with potato chips, or pāpad and Raita (page 165) or plain unsweetened dairy-free yogurt.
- Any leftovers can be stored in the refrigerator for up to 2 days.
- Reheat in the microwave or on the stovetop.

Lehsuni Palak Khichdi

Comforting meal of rice and lentils cooked together with spice and garlic-infused pureed spinach

Ask any Indian why they love khichdi (yes, everyone does), and their response will be one or all of these—it is simple, comforting, wholesome and delicious. Every Indian state has its own version of the preparation (I know, I keep saying this throughout this book. But hey, it is true!), but the general recipe always includes rice, lentils, spices and a simple tadkā. Deriving its origins from khicca in Sanskrit, khichdi loosely translates into a combination of lentils and rice. It can be spicy or plain, made with a single type of lentil or a combination. Perfect for chilly days, rainy days, sick days, back-from-vacation days or even days when you are craving something soothing and effortless. This version has pureed spinach and spices flavored with garlic (lehsuni)—a version quite popular in Indian restaurants.

*Yield: 2 to 4 servings * Prep Time: 10 minutes * Cook Time: 45 minutes*

1 cup (200 g) basmati rice

½ cup (100 g) moong dāl (split moong/mung beans)

½ tsp ground turmeric (haldi powder)

2 tsp (12 g) salt, or to taste

6 cups (180 g) fresh baby spinach

½ bunch of fresh cilantro

2 green chili peppers, or according to taste

1-inch (2.5-cm) piece fresh ginger

To a bowl, add the basmati rice and moong dāl. Wash them thoroughly under running water, rubbing them with your fingers. Do this two to three times until the water appears fairly clear.

Boil about 3 cups (720 ml) of water in a kettle or a pot on the stovetop. This will be used to cook the khichdi and to thin it out, if needed, at a later step.

To a pressure cooker, add the washed rice, moong dāl, ground turmeric and salt, along with 4 cups (960 ml) of water. Pressure cook on low for 7 to 10 minutes. Once the pressure is naturally released, open the pressure cooker. If you do not have a pressure cooker, cook the rice and dāl on the stovetop in a large nonstick saucepan with enough water. Cook until the rice and dāl are completely cooked through and all the water is absorbed. Overall cooking time will vary, as pressure-cooking method is much faster.

To cook the spinach, add about 5 cups (1L) water in a large stockpot or saucepan, and bring it to a boil.

Meanwhile, prepare a bowl with a few ice cubes and 2 cups (480 ml) of water.

Now salt the water in the stockpot with the boiling water, and add the spinach. Blanch the spinach for 30 seconds. Immediately remove the spinach using a pair of tongs and add it to the ice bath. After about a minute, remove the spinach leaves and transfer them to a blender. Add the cilantro, green chili peppers and ginger, and process until smooth and creamy.

(continued)

Lehsuni Palak Khichdi (continued)

2 tbsp (30 ml) neutral oil, divided

1 tsp cumin seeds (jeera)

Pinch of hing (asafoetida)

4 cloves garlic, minced, plus 3 cloves garlic thinly sliced for tadkā

1 whole dried red chili

1 small red onion, finely chopped

1 medium tomato, diced

1½ tsp (3 g) ground coriander (dhaniya powder)

2 tsp (4 g) ground garam masālā (homemade [see page 165] or store-bought)

½ tsp Kashmiri red chili powder

Roasted unsalted cashews, optional, for serving

Heat 1 tablespoon (15 ml) of the oil in a skillet over medium heat. Add the cumin seeds, hing, 4 cloves of the garlic and the whole dried red chili, and sauté until the garlic is fragrant, about 30 seconds. Stir in the onion, season with salt, and cook until the onion turns pink. Add the tomato, ground coriander and garam masālā, and cook until the tomato turns mushy, about 5 minutes.

Add ½ cup (120 ml) of hot water, and continue to cook for a minute. Then add the blended spinach. Cook, stirring often, for 5 minutes. Add this to the cooked rice and dāl mixture along with ½ cup (120 ml) of hot water. You may add more or less depending on your preference. Stir well to combine, and cook on low for 5 minutes, stirring often. Turn off the heat.

Heat the remaining 1 tablespoon (15 ml) of oil in the same skillet, and add the remaining 3 cloves garlic. Cook until the garlic turns light brown. Turn off the heat, sprinkle with the Kashmiri red chili powder, and pour the tadkā into the prepared khichdi. Top with roasted cashews, if using. Cover until ready to serve.

How to Enjoy

- Serve piping-hot with Silky Punjabi Kadhi with Pakoda (page 85), achār/Indian-style pickle or Raita (page 165) or plain unsweetened dairy-free yogurt on the side along with pāpad.

- To reheat, transfer the khichdi to a saucepan, add hot boiling water a little at a time to get the right consistency, and simmer for 3 to 4 minutes. You can prepare a fresh tadkā (tempering) and pour it over the top. Microwave reheating is not recommended.

Tip

You may use brown rice for a heartier meal, but the cooking time and the quantity of water will vary.

Bold Bhindi Masālā

Fried okra in a creamy tomato-onion gravy

I am one of those people who always get stressed out when someone is coming over for a meal. I usually end up making several dishes, and continue to worry if all that food would suffice. Bhindi Masālā is one of my go-to Indian recipes for entertaining because it is quick and simple to whip-up, although it makes my guests think I have spent a lot of time in my kitchen to prepare it. Bhindi, okra in Hindi, is everybody's favorite. The key is to fry the okra well to make sure you get the most flavor out of this vegetable while avoiding a slimy texture.

Yield: 4 servings ✳ *Prep Time: 20 minutes* ✳ *Cook Time: 40 minutes*

1 lb (454 g) fresh okra

6 tbsp (90 ml) neutral oil, divided

1 tsp cumin seeds (jeera)

1 tbsp (6 g) fresh ginger, grated

3 cloves garlic, peeled and minced

2 medium onions (any color), thinly sliced

Salt, to taste

½ tsp ground turmeric (haldi powder)

1 tsp red chili powder or cayenne pepper, or use according to taste

1 tbsp (6 g) ground coriander (dhaniya powder)

1 tsp āmchur powder (dry mango powder)

3 medium tomatoes, finely diced

⅓ cup (180 ml) plain unsweetened dairy free yogurt, whisked

1 cup (240 ml) hot water

Wash and thoroughly pat dry the okra with a kitchen towel. Cut off the crowns and the tips, and cut the okra into 2-inch (5-cm) pieces.

In a large skillet over medium-high heat, heat 4 tablespoons (60 ml) of the oil. Shallow fry the okra until they shrink and appear slightly charred around the edges, about 12 minutes.

Transfer the okra to a plate, and set it aside.

In the same skillet over medium-high heat, heat the remaining 2 tablespoons (30 ml) of oil. Add the cumin seeds, and cook until they sizzle. Add the ginger, garlic, sliced onions, salt, ground turmeric, red chili powder, ground coriander and āmchur powder, and sauté, stirring frequently, until the onions appear slightly brown, about 7 minutes. Add a splash of water if needed to prevent the spices from burning.

Stir in the tomatoes, cover, and cook over medium heat for 3 to 4 minutes, or until the tomatoes appear mushy.

Uncover the skillet, reduce the heat to the lowest setting, and stir in the whisked yogurt. Continue to cook over low heat for another 2 minutes, until you notice oil on the sides of the skillet.

Add about ½ cup (120 ml) of water (adjust quantity to desired consistency), and bring the gravy to a gentle simmer for a minute.

Add the fried okra, mix gently, cover, and cook over medium-low heat for 5 to 7 minutes.

(continued)

Bold Bhindi Masala *(continued)*

1 medium tomato, cut into large pieces

1 medium onion, cut into large petals

1 tsp garam masālā (homemade [see page 165] or store-bought)

1 tsp kasuri methi (dried fenugreek leaves), crushed

Fresh cilantro, to serve

Stir in the tomato, onion, garam masālā, and kasuri methi in quick succession. The onions and tomatoes added at this stage need to retain their shape and texture.

Check for seasoning and adjust, if needed.

Add the fresh cilantro, and turn off heat.

How to Enjoy

- Serve hot with Layered Triangle Parātha (page 66) or any flatbread and Raita (page 165).
- Store any leftovers in an airtight container in the refrigerator.
- Reheat in a skillet or microwave, and serve immediately. If the gravy appears thick, add a few spoonfuls of hot water while reheating.

Tips

- *Be sure to use fresh, tender okra for this recipe. The tail of the fresh okra pods should snap easily and not bend.*
- *Make sure the okra is dried thoroughly before using in this recipe.*

Effortless Dadpe Pohe

Spiced coconut-y rice flakes

My brother has only one answer to the question "What do you want for breakfast?" The answer is always poha. I must admit, the reasons are good enough for wanting to eat poha often—it is quick, filling, made with basic pantry ingredients and, most important, it tastes good. There are different versions of poha across India—some made with onions, some with onions and potatoes. A quick version with just chili peppers and lemon juice is something I make often when I run out of ideas for the lunch box. Indori poha is one of my favorites; it is sweet, spicy and topped with crunchy sev. But I am sharing a lesser-known version of poha called dadpe pohe (pohe is poha in Marathi) that belongs to the Konkan part of the western state of Maharashtra.

Yield: 3 to 4 servings * *Prep Time: 10 minutes* * *Cook Time: 20 minutes*

4 cups (170 g) thin poha (flattened rice) (see Tips)

1 medium red onion, finely chopped (about 1 cup [160 g])

¾ cup (75 g) unsweetened, shredded coconut (fresh or frozen), see Tips

1 tsp salt, or to taste

1 tsp granulated sugar

1 cup (240 ml) unflavored coconut water

3 tbsp (45 ml) neutral oil

1 tsp black mustard seeds (rāi)

Pinch of hing (asafoetida)

1 tsp ground turmeric (haldi powder)

3 green chili peppers, or according to taste, finely chopped

3 tbsp (40 g) roasted unsalted peanuts

Finely chopped fresh cilantro

2 to 3 tbsp (30 to 45 ml) fresh lemon juice

In a large bowl, mix the poha, onion, coconut, salt, sugar and coconut water. Set it aside for about 10 minutes.

In a small tadkā pan or skillet, heat the oil over medium heat until it glistens. Add the black mustard seeds, and once they begin to pop, after about a minute, add the hing. Once the popping of the seeds stops, turn off the heat and add the ground turmeric, green chili peppers, peanuts and cilantro immediately to the skillet.

Give it a quick stir, and add it to the bowl with the poha. Immediately cover the bowl with a lid, and keep it covered for at least 5 minutes. This is an important step; the steam from the tadkā helps to further soften the poha.

Add the fresh lemon juice, stir well to combine, and cover for another 5 minutes before serving.

How to Enjoy

- This dish is perfect for breakfast or an early lunch. Serve with a cup of Invigorating Masālā Chāi (page 143).
- If you can find mirgunda (pappadāms made with poha) in any South Asian grocery store near you, you are in luck! Fry them up and serve them along with dadpe pohe.

Tips
- *You can use fresh or frozen grated coconut (not desiccated). Frozen grated coconut is easily available in most South Asian stores. Just remember to thaw a small quantity needed for the recipe in advance. You may also take the quantity needed for a recipe and then microwave it for about 30 seconds to a minute for quicker thawing.*
- *For this recipe, you will need "thin" poha since we are not cooking the poha over the heat. Look for a pack that specifically says "thin poha."*

Lip-Smacking Gobi Bhuna

Spiced cauliflower and bell pepper gravy

Fresh spices are key here, which is why this dish is packed with flavor. Gobi is cauliflower, and bhuna is a technique of cooking, which means to fry the base masālā until it starts to caramelize and gives out oil along the sides. The taste of the parātha and gobi bhuna that I had in New Delhi still stays with me to this day.

Yield: 4 servings ✳ *Prep Time: 15 minutes* ✳ *Cook Time: 1 hour*

2 tbsp (30 ml) neutral oil

2 (1-inch [2.5-cm]) cinnamon sticks (dālchini)

3 whole cloves (lavang)

2 whole green cardamom pods (elaichi)

½ tsp fennel seeds (saunf)

1 large red onion, sliced

Salt, to taste

1 tbsp (6 g) fresh ginger, grated

4 cloves garlic, minced

1 green chili pepper, or according to taste, finely chopped

2 medium ripe tomatoes, finely diced

1 tsp tomato paste

1 tsp ground turmeric (haldi powder)

1 tsp Kashmiri red chili powder, or according to taste

1 tsp ground cumin (jeera powder)

1 tbsp (6 g) ground coriander (dhaniya powder)

1 medium head cauliflower, cut into florets

1 large green bell pepper, sliced into long strips

Handful of fresh cilantro leaves, chopped

1 tbsp (14 g) kasuri methi (dry fenugreek leaves), crushed

Heat the oil in a wide skillet over medium heat. Add the cinnamon sticks, whole cloves, cardamom pods and fennel seeds, and sauté for 1 minute or until fragrant.

Add the onion and salt, and sauté until the onion turns light brown, about 2 minutes. Add the ginger, garlic, green chili pepper and tomatoes, and cook until the tomatoes soften, 3 to 4 minutes. Stir in the tomato paste, ground turmeric, Kashmiri red chili powder, ground cumin and ground coriander, and continue to cook for about 8 minutes, or until the raw aroma of the spices and the tomato paste disappears.

Add the cauliflower florets and about 1½ cups (360 ml) of water to the skillet, then cover, reduce the heat to medium-low, and cook for 12 minutes, until you see a layer of oil floating on the surface of the gravy.

Uncover and check the cauliflower stalks for doneness. When they are fork-tender, add the bell pepper, and simmer for just 2 minutes. Sprinkle in the fresh cilantro and kasuri methi, mix well to combine, and turn off heat. Remove and discard the cinnamon sticks, whole cloves and cardamom pods.

How to Enjoy

Serve hot with Layered Triangle Parātha (page 66) or any flatbread, along with thinly sliced onions.

Tips

- *Add hot water to adjust the consistency after the cauliflower is cooked, if needed. If you like it thicker, simmer uncovered for longer; if you prefer thinner gravy, add more hot water and simmer for 2 minutes.*
- *You can buy whole spices online or at any South Asian grocery store. Store whole spices in an airtight container.*

Treats: A Little Something Special

Everyone loves a delicious dessert, but sometimes you don't want too much of it. Indian sweets are known to be rich and indulgent. One of the main reasons for this is the heavy use of dairy in many popular sweets that use milk, cream and ghee. All the sweet treats in this chapter are dairy-free, of course, and you can make them with little to no effort. Some of them are healthy-ish, some are a bit rich because of the use of nuts. A few require a bit of planning ahead, like Special Pansache Dhonas (page 160) and Cooling Kesar Kulfi (page 140), but they all require only a few ingredients. All of them are as satisfying as they are easy to make.

Royal Qubani ka Meetha

Stewed apricot with ice cream

The name of the dessert derives from Urdu language, which loosely translates to qubani meaning "apricot" and meetha meaning "sweet." Qubani ka meetha is traditionally prepared with dried apricots, which are deseeded and soaked overnight. Then they are cooked in sugar and water until the apricots turn soft and mushy. The final product is decadent and aromatic, and while vanilla ice cream is not the classic pairing, in my opinion, a good-quality vegan vanilla ice cream takes this already delicious dessert to another level of deliciousness.

Yield: 4 to 6 servings ✳ Prep Time: 5 minutes ✳ Cook Time: 45 minutes

1 cup (170 g) dried apricots, roughly chopped and soaked in ½ cup (120 ml) warm water for 4 to 5 hours

¼ cup (50 g) granulated sugar

Pinch of saffron (kesar)

⅛ tsp food-grade rose water, optional

Unsalted almonds, toasted, chopped, or slivered, for serving

Vegan vanilla ice cream, for serving

Edible dried rose petals, for serving, optional

In a saucepan, add the soaked dried apricots, along with the water in which they were soaking, followed by another 1½ cups (360 ml) of water and the sugar.

Bring the ingredients to a gentle simmer for about 30 minutes, stirring occasionally.

Stir in the saffron, and continue to simmer, mashing the apricots pieces, for another 10 minutes so that the consistency is jam-like. You may need to add a few drops of water if the consistency appears too thick.

Turn off the heat; add the rose water, if using, and the almonds.

How to Enjoy

Serve warm or chilled with vegan vanilla ice cream and edible dried rose petals, if desired.

Tip

Qubani ka meetha can be made in advance and stored in the refrigerator for about three days. Make sure you add the toppings like nuts, rose petals or the ice cream just before serving.

Cooling Kesar Kulfi

India's favorite frozen indulgence with saffron and nuts

I did not live in India for very long, but I've always heard from friends and cousins and seen in the movies about how on a hot summer day all you wish for is something sweet, refreshing and icy. And at that exact moment, serendipitously, a kulfi vala (kulfi vendor) will appear! A creamy and luxurious no-churn treat, it is a not only a summer favorite, but enjoyed throughout the year. It melts beautifully, so when you are almost getting done with the serving, you are left with a small pool of creamy deliciousness and some crunchy bits of nuts on the plate. And of course, the amazing flavors of cardamom and saffron in your mouth. Kulfi is traditionally dairy-based, but this guilt-free version gives you all those delicious flavors and textures of a traditional one without the dairy.

Yield: 6 servings ✳ *Prep Time: 10 minutes* ✳ *Cook Time: 1 hour (plus freezing time)*

¾ cup (100 g) raw unsalted cashews, soaked in hot water for 15 minutes

4 cups (960 ml) full-fat unsweetened plant milk, divided (see Tip)

6 tbsp (90 g) granulated sugar

1 tbsp (6 g) ground cardamom (elaichi)

Generous pinch of saffron strands (kesar)

1 heaping tbsp (8 g) roasted, unsalted, chopped pistachios

1 heaping tbsp (9 g) roasted, unsalted, chopped almonds

Drain the water from the cashews, and blend them with 2 cups (480 ml) of the unsweetened plant-based milk to a smooth paste. Set aside.

In a saucepan, add the blended cashews and the remaining 2 cups (480 ml) of milk, and bring them to a boil in a over medium heat, stirring occasionally and scraping the sides of the pan to remove any solidified milk, if required. Continue cooking for about 40 minutes.

Stir in the sugar, ground cardamom, saffron, pistachios and almonds, and cook for another minute or until the sugar is completely dissolved. Turn off the heat, and let the mixture cool completely. Cover the mixture after 10 minutes.

Pour the mixture into Popsicle® or kulfi molds, and freeze them for at least 6 to 8 hours. You may also pour it into a glass baking dish, cover and freeze it to scoop and serve in cups.

How to Enjoy

If using a kulfi mold, unmold and serve on a plate with some additional nuts sprinkled on top, if you like.

Tip
Any full-fat unsweetened plant milk except coconut works well. Even better if you can find one that says "extra-creamy." Oat and almond milk are the best options.

Invigorating Masālā Chāi

Traditional Indian tea spiced with masālā

Chāi has deep roots in Indian and South Asian culture. There are a lot of misconceptions about chāi, and I am sure you already know about the most common one. Chāi is the word for tea in Hindi, so when people mistakenly say "chāi tea," they are actually saying "tea tea." The chāi that I used to enjoy occasionally as a teenager was karak, a tea made with black tea leaves, cardamom and evaporated milk, commonly found in many countries outside India, like the UAE, Qatar, etc. In India, the first time I had chāi, it was the cutting chāi that my friends introduced me to. Strong, delicious, piping-hot chāi, but served in special small glasses, it was basically a half order of chāi, often implying a single order that is shared among friends. Less quantity means you can enjoy multiple glasses spread throughout the day! I am a coffee drinker, but my husband loves a cup of chāi every day, and this masālā-infused chāi with jaggery is the first thing he thinks about when he wakes up. There are many variations of the kind of spices that are added to chāi. Every family has their unique chāi recipe. So even though the base flavor of chāi is the same, the masālās added to the pot while brewing the chāi are what define the flavor. This is my favorite way to make it for friends and family. It's special because of the addition of saffron and rose petals. If you don't have access to these items, feel free to omit them. The chāi will taste just as delicious.

*Yield: 2 servings * Prep Time: 5 minutes * Cook Time: 10 minutes*

1-inch (2.5-cm) piece fresh ginger

½ tsp fennel seeds (saunf)

2 green cardamom pods (elaichi)

2½ tbsp (5 g) loose black tea leaves

Jaggery powder or raw sugar, according to taste

1 cup (240 ml) unsweetened plant milk of choice (preferably oat or soy)

2 tsp (2 g) edible dried rose petals, optional

2 pinches of saffron (kesar), optional

1 tsp food-grade rose water, optional

Tips

- *For a true taste of masālā chāi, choose a full-bodied, strong, black loose-leaf tea.*
- *If you would like a stronger flavor, simmer the chāi for longer.*

Prepare the chāi masālā (spice blend) by crushing the ginger, fennel seeds and cardamom pods using a mortar and pestle or a rolling pin.

Add the crushed spices and 1 cup (240 ml) of water to a medium saucepan, and simmer on low for about 5 minutes, or until fragrant and the water is a deep, amber color. This process lets the spices fully infuse into the water. Add the tea leaves, stir in the jaggery and continue to simmer for 3 to 4 minutes.

Add the plant milk, increase the heat to medium-high and bring the mixture to a boil for about 3 minutes, until the mixture is the color of caramel. During this process, using a ladle, scoop some chāi and pour it back into the saucepan to create bubbles. This process is called chāi-pulling and it helps aerate the chāi, developing its flavor.

Let the chāi boil to the brim (keep your eyes on the pot!) for about another 3 minutes.

Turn off the heat, and add the rose petals, saffron and rose water, if using. Strain the chāi into a teapot or mugs, and serve piping-hot

How to Enjoy

Serve hot with some fun snacks like Crunchy Makhāna (page 24), The Iconic Vada Pav (page 19), Spongy Ravā Dhokla (page 27) or Everybody's Favorite Kānda Bhajiya with Special Onion Chutney (page 23).

Filling Khajur-Kaju Smoothie

Thick and creamy blend of dates and cashews in oat milk

This thick and creamy concoction is made with dates, cashews and plant milk. The sweet dates give the smoothie a rich, caramel flavor. Growing up in the Middle East, I was familiar with many varieties of dates, and I remember having chilled glasses of jellab at Lebanese restaurants. The first time I had a date smoothie in a small restaurant in Mumbai, it transported me back to my childhood days of jellab. With the heat and humidity on high in the city, this drink was the much-needed cooler. It was refreshing and downright delicious and is now a summer staple in my house.

Yield: 2 servings ✳ *Prep Time: 5 minutes* ✳ *Cook Time: 5 minutes*

10 to 12 pitted Medjool dates, or any soft variety

½ cup (70 g) unsalted raw unsalted cashews, plus more for serving

1½ cups (360 ml) unsweetened plant-based milk of choice

2 to 3 ice cubes

4 tbsp (60 ml) cashew cream, divided (page 164) or use any variety of unsweetened dairy-free cream

Date syrup, for serving, optional

In a blender, combine the dates, cashews, milk and ice cubes, and blend until smooth and creamy. Pour into glasses, and top each glass with 2 tablespoons (30 ml) of the cashew cream. Serve with date syrup, if using, and some cashews.

How to Enjoy

- Serve chilled.
- You can freeze the serving glasses an hour before using them for a truly refreshing treat.

Tips

- *Softer varieties of dates are easier to process. If you have a drier, tougher variety, soak them in warm water and blend them. You may soak the cashews in warm water as well before blending.*
- *Add more or less of the dates to suit your preference. Some varieties of dates are sweeter than others. Taste them before you decide the quantity you want to use for the recipe.*

Simple Āte ka Halva

Whole wheat fudge

The best thing about this halva, apart from being delicious, is how easy it is to make. It is one of those recipes that is made in minutes and devoured in seconds. When made the traditional way, in gurudwaras, or home kitchens, the cooking time is long. My mom and I found a microwave recipe for this in a magazine years ago, and this has been my go-to quick dessert ever since. The only change I made after going vegan is substituting fruity olive oil for ghee, and it works beautifully. Āta means "flour" (whole wheat flour in this case), and halva is a fudge-like sweet treat. Halva can be amped up with a variety of additions like nuts and edible rose petals. For a quick treat, I leave it plain and rustic, but occasionally I make it fancy like this recipe. This microwave version is perfect for lazy days. My beloved dog, Neo (who loves this halva), agrees.

---

*Yield: 4 to 6 servings * Prep Time: 5 minutes * Cook Time: 10 minutes*

---

1 cup (120 g) whole wheat flour (gehun ka āta)

½ cup (120 ml) fruity extra-virgin olive oil

1 cup (200 g) granulated sugar

2 tsp (4 g) ground cardamom (elaichi powder)

Toasted chopped or slivered unsalted almonds, for garnish

Edible dried rose petals, for garnish, optional

In a medium-sized, microwave-safe bowl, mix the flour and the olive oil. Microwave the mixture for 3 minutes, stopping every minute to stir the contents of the bowl to ensure the flour doesn't burn. The color of the flour should be medium brown because of the microwave roasting process.

Add the sugar, ground cardamom and about 1 cup (240 ml) water. Whisk well to make sure there are no lumps, and microwave for 2 minutes more or until the sugar is dissolved.

Remove the bowl carefully from the microwave, and stir once. Top with nuts and/or edible rose petals, if using.

How to Enjoy

- Serve warm.
- The halva can be reheated in the microwave.

Tips

- *You can also set the halva in a greased tray right after you remove it from the microwave by gentling pressing the halva down with a spatula. Then score the halva into squares using a paring knife, and sprinkle the toppings for a beautiful presentation.*
- *The halva does not need time to set in the tray. It will start firming up slightly and taking shape as it sits in the tray.*

Luxurious Pista Lassi

Pistachio-flavored yogurt-based smoothie

Smooth and creamy, lassi (pronounced as luh-see, not "lassie") is a luxurious refresher. Its origins are said to be in the Punjab region of the subcontinent, but lassis are now found everywhere, from street stalls to fancy restaurants. It is a simple creation but truly versatile. A classic sweet lassi (there is also a salty variation) consists of thick yogurt whisked with sugar, water and ice cubes. Traditional lassi shops in Punjab top their lassi with makhan (butter) and malai (cream) and whisk the lassi with milk instead of water. This light, plant-based version tastes just as delicious and is a perfect pick-me-up for any time of the day. Everybody loves mango lassi, but I love the unique flavor and texture of the pistachio lassi.

Yield: 1 serving ✳ *Prep Time: 5 minutes* ✳ *Cook Time: 5 minutes*

¾ cup (180 ml) plain, unsweetened dairy-free yogurt

¼ cup (25 g) unsalted roasted coarsely chopped pistachios, plus more for serving

1¾ tbsp (25 g) granulated sugar

2 ice cubes

2 tbsp (30 ml) dairy-free heavy cream, optional

¼ cup (60 ml) cold water (optional, if needed to thin yogurt)

Generous pinch of saffron, plus a couple strands for serving

In a blender, combine the yogurt, pistachios, sugar, ice cubes and heavy cream, if using. Blend until smooth and creamy. You may need to add some cold water depending on the consistency of the yogurt. The lassi should be the consistency of a milkshake.

How to Enjoy

Pour into a glass, sprinkle with additional pistachios and the saffron strands, if using, and serve chilled.

Tips

- *The lassi can be refrigerated for a few hours before serving. Just add the toppings before serving.*
- *Make sure you are using plain, unsweetened, dairy-free yogurt. If you do not have an unsweetened variety (it is sometimes hard to find one), reduce or eliminate the sugar in the preparation.*
- *You can buy roasted unsalted nuts or roast them at home in a skillet or the microwave. Just make sure you don't roast them for too long. You will need a mortar and pestle or a heavy skillet to crush them once they are toasted.*

Energizing Pazham Nurukku

Caramelized plantains with jaggery

One of the most fascinating characteristics of Kerala cuisine is the versatile use of bananas and plantains. Pazham means "banana" and the "zh" is pronounced with a soft "r" sound. Sweet plantains are bananas' cousins. They are starchy, robust and a powerhouse of nutrients. They are used in stews, gravies, jams, snacks (my favorite is the addictive nendrakai chips—lightly salted plantain chips) and desserts. Pazham nurukku is a traditional Kerala preparation where sweet, ripe plantains called nendran pazham are seared in coconut oil until caramelized, and then coated in melted jaggery.

Yield: 1 to 2 servings ✳ *Prep Time: 5 minutes* ✳ *Cook Time: 20 minutes*

1 tbsp (14 g) coconut oil

2 ripe plantains, cut into thick coins

1 tsp ground cardamom (elaichi powder)

3 tbsp (60 g) powdered or grated jaggery (gur)

¼ cup (60 ml) full-fat coconut milk from a can

Heat the coconut oil in a nonstick skillet over medium heat, and add the plantain coins. Cook for 2 minutes until caramelized. Gently flip and cook the other side until it appears golden brown. Turn off the heat.

Sprinkle with the ground cardamom and powdered jaggery, and drizzle with the coconut milk before serving.

How to Enjoy

Serve warm as breakfast or a post-workout snack.

Tip

Plantains are sold in the fresh produce section of well-stocked grocery stores. You may find them in international farmers markets or South Asian stores as well. To select the perfect ones for this recipe, look for those with brown, mottled skin.

Fabulous Falooda

Rose-flavored milk with vermicelli and basil seeds

If you are familiar with Filipino halo-halo or the Vietnamese che, then you'll know what to expect from falooda. Falooda is a rose-flavored dessert loved in India and other South Asian countries. Falooda is not native to India, but it has evolved from faloodeh, a much-beloved treat of Iran. The fragrant, bright red rose syrup is a staple in many South Asian homes, sometimes diluted with chilled water to provide relief from all the heat and humidity. In falooda, the chilled rose-flavored milk is layered with fruit jelly, soft and delicate corn vermicelli, and basil seeds, and is crowned with a big scoop of any type of ice cream. Falooda is one of the first things I ever made when I was in high school. My parents had invited a few of their friends for a meal, and everybody enjoyed this delicious dessert-drink.

*Yield: 2 tall glasses * Prep Time: 10 minutes * Cook Time: 15 minutes*

2 tbsp (20 g) tukmaria (raw basil seeds), soaked in 1 cup (240 ml) water (see Tips)

2 packs vegan gelatin powder (strawberry or raspberry flavored), prepared according to package instructions, set and chilled in a tray

About 1 cup (140 g) of falooda sev (corn vermicelli or rice vermicelli), prepared according to package instructions

4 tbsp (60 ml) rose syrup, divided, plus more for drizzling (see Tips)

3½ cups (840 ml) unsweetened plant-based milk of choice (such as creamy almond or oat)

Dairy-free vanilla ice cream for serving

Unsalted almonds and/or pistachios, for serving

Dried edible rose petals, for serving, optional

In a small bowl, stir together 1 cup (240 ml) of cold water and the tukmaria; let the seeds soak until the water is absorbed, about 10 minutes. Drain them and set the seeds aside until ready to assemble.

Remove the set gelatin from the refrigerator. Run a knife along edges of the pan. Flip the pan over; gently tap the bottom to release the gelatin. Cut the gelatin into ½- to ¾-inch (1- to 2-cm) cubes. Set aside to cool in the refrigerator until ready to assemble.

Boil the falooda sev according to the package instructions. Drain them into a colander, and rinse them with cold water. Set them aside until ready to assemble.

To assemble the falooda, in a tall glass, add a few spoonfuls of the tukmaria. Top with a few strands of cooked falooda sev, followed by a few gelatin cubes. Add about 2 tablespoons (30 ml) of rose syrup into each glass. Pour some milk over the rose syrup. Top the glasses with a scoop of vanilla ice cream, a drizzle of rose syrup, unsalted nuts and rose petals, if using.

How to Enjoy

Serve in tall, chilled glasses with a straw and a tall spoon.

Tips

- *You can make this ahead by preparing every component of the falooda separately and storing it in the refrigerator until you are ready for assembly.*
- *Tukmaria/raw basil seeds can be substituted with chia seeds. Just soak the chia seeds in water, then drain before use.*
- *Falooda sev is found in most South Asian grocery stores. If you don't have access to falooda sev, you can use rice vermicelli.*
- *Rose syrup is bright red, flavored sweetened syrup that is available in most South Asian stores in a tall bottle.*

Nutty Rose Ladoos

Sugar-free sweet treats with rose petal jam

Ladoos are mithais (sweet treats in Hindi) that are shaped into balls. There are many types of ladoos, ranging from milk-based ones that are rolled in grated coconut to saffron-colored ones made with boondi (fried, sweetened chickpea flour balls). This ladoo is sugar-free, loaded with nuts, has a chewy texture because of the dates, and is topped with gulkand, rose petal jam. I tasted this for the first time a few years ago at a popular mithai shop in Mumbai. The rose petals in which the laddus were rolled is what caught my attention. To my luck, it happened to be the only vegan mithai in the entire store. This is a re-creation of that delicious treat.

Yield: 10 to 12 ladoos ✳ *Prep Time: 10 minutes* ✳ *Cook Time: 50 minutes*

1 tbsp (15 ml) neutral oil

½ cup (70 g) unsalted almonds, coarsely chopped

½ cup (70 g) unsalted cashews, coarsely chopped

¼ cup (30 g) unsalted, shelled pistachios, coarsely chopped

2 tbsp (28 g) unsalted walnuts, coarsely chopped

½ cup (87 g) soft, pitted dates, such as Medjool

¼ cup (160 g) rose petal jam (gulkand) (see Tips)

½ tbsp (3 g) ground cardamom (elaichi)

¾ cup (30 g) edible dried rose petals, optional (see Tips)

In a large skillet over medium heat, add the oil, and roast the almonds for 3 to 4 minutes, stirring continuously. Once they turn slightly golden, transfer them to a plate.

To the same skillet, add the cashews, roast them for 2 to 3 minutes, or until light brown, and transfer to the same plate with the roasted almonds.

To the same skillet, add the pistachios and walnuts together, and lightly toast for 3 to 4 minutes, stirring continuously. Transfer to the plate.

While the nuts are cooling, in a food processor, process the dates with the rose petal jam and ground cardamom. Add the processed dates and rose petal jam to the plate with the nuts, and mix everything until well combined.

Prepare a plate with some edible rose petals, if using. Take a small portion of the nut mixture, and roll it into a ball. Roll the balls into the rose petals a couple of times so that the petals stick to the surface of the balls.

How to Enjoy

- Serve on a platter.
- Store ladoos in an airtight container, and refrigerate for up to a week.

Tips

- *Gulkand is available in well-stocked South Asian grocery stores. You may also find it at Persian stores where they are called morabayeh goleh sorkh. The consistency of the jam and the sweet content may differ. You may need to adjust the quantity of the jam depending on the type you get.*
- *Edible dried rose petals are available in most well-stocked South Asian or Persian stores, international markets or online specialty stores.*

Luscious Mango Mastāni

Pune-famous creamy mango milkshake

Seasonal fresh mangoes are used to make mastāni, a thick and creamy milkshake, but they are not always available. I am sure whoever has had the Alphonso variety of mangoes would agree—they are the best-tasting ones, because they are a perfect blend of buttery texture and floral aroma. They make the best-tasting mango mastāni, too. There is nothing quite like fresh Indian mangoes, but when you can't find them, the next best thing is the canned variety. This way you can enjoy creamy deliciousness year-round. The perfect mastāni should be thick enough for a spoon to stand in but still drinkable.

Yield: 4 to 6 servings ✳ *Prep Time: 10 minutes* ✳ *Cook Time: 15 minutes*

1 (30-oz [850-g]) chilled can mango pulp (āmras) (see Tips)

1½ cups (360 ml) unsweetened plant-based milk of choice, plus more as needed

3 heaping scoops dairy-free vanilla ice cream

2 to 3 ice cubes

2 tsp (4 g) ground cardamom (elaichi)

Seasonal fresh mango (any variety), peeled, pit removed and diced, for serving

Dairy-free mango sorbet or dairy-free vanilla ice cream, for serving, optional

A few strands of saffron (kesar), for serving, optional

Unsalted almonds or pistachios, roasted and coarsely chopped, for serving

Maraschino cherries, for serving, optional

In a blender, combine the mango pulp, 1½ cups (360 ml) of the milk, the ice cream, ice cubes and ground cardamom. Add up to ¼ cup (60 ml) more milk by the tablespoon (15 ml) for a thinner consistency, if desired. Pour into glasses. and top with fresh mango, sorbet, if using, saffron, if using, almonds and/or maraschino cherries, if desired.

How to Enjoy

Mastāni is served chilled.

Tips

- *Āmras is available in cans in most Indian grocery stores. Look for one that says "kesar" or "alphonso" mango pulp. These are the best varieties for a mastāni. 24 Mantra, Laxmi and Deep are some of the commonly found canned mango pulp brands.*

- *Use any variety of dairy-free vanilla ice cream except one that is coconut milk-based.*

- *You can make the basic mastāni in advance and store it in the refrigerator for use later. Add the toppings just before serving. Saffron can be overpowering. If using, a couple of strands per glass is good.*

Succulent Jalebi

Crispy, chewy, saffron-flavored treats

Jalebi is a sweet treat in India popularly served with a savory breakfast in many parts of the country. Two unforgettable jalebi combinations I had during my travels were jalebi and hing kachori in Mathura, and jalebi and poha in Indore. Jalabi is a Persian import, a version of zolabiya, a festive treat from Iran. The traditional way of making jalebi takes some time and patience; the batter is ground and then fermented overnight. Ghee is the cooking medium in many places, but oil is also commonly used. This method of adding baking soda or fruit salt is perfect for instant gratification. The classic traditional jalebi—served in the streets of India, made fresh by halwais (professional confectioners) without the use of fancy piping bags or squirt bottles, but just a pouch made of muslin cloth that is filled with the batter—is truly the best.

*Yield: 4 servings * Prep Time: 40 minutes * Cook Time: 30 minutes*

1 cup (125 g) all-purpose flour

½ tsp baking soda

1 tsp cornstarch

2 tbsp (30 ml) plain, unsweetened, dairy-free yogurt

Neutral oil, for deep-frying

1½ cups (300 g) granulated sugar

4 saffron strands (kesar strands)

1 tbsp (15 ml) lemon juice

Unsalted roasted pistachios, coarsely chopped, for serving

Tips

• *To test if the oil is ready for frying, squeeze a drop of batter into it. If it immediately starts to bubble and rise to the surface, it is perfect. If the batter browns immediately, it is too hot. If it drops to the bottom of the skillet, the oil is not hot enough.*

• *To check for one-string consistency, dip a spoon into the syrup, and let it cool for a few seconds. Lightly rub the syrup between your thumb and index finger, and pull the fingers apart; if you see a single string, the syrup is ready.*

In a large bowl, combine the all-purpose flour, baking soda, cornstarch and yogurt. Pour about ½ cup (120 ml) water, a little at a time, to make a thick batter, like that of a pancake. Whisk the batter continuously for 5 to 7 minutes to incorporate air into the mixture. Set the batter aside for 15 minutes.

Heat oil in a deep skillet, about halfway up the sides, over medium heat.

While the oil is heating, make the sugar syrup in a wide saucepan. Combine the sugar, about 1 cup (240 ml) water and the saffron. Cook until the sugar has completely dissolved, and then continue to cook until the sugar has a one-string consistency (see Tips), about 5 more minutes, 15 minutes in total. Stir in the lemon juice, reduce the heat to low, and keep the sugar syrup warm.

Whisk the batter once again thoroughly for 5 minutes.

Transfer the batter to a piping bag or a squeeze bottle. Gently pipe the batter into the hot (approximately 320°F [160°C]) oil, close to the surface to create a spiral shape that is 2 to 3 inches (5 to 8 cm) wide. Cook for 2 to 3 minutes, gently flip, and cook for another minute, or until golden brown.

Remove the jalebi from the oil using a slotted spoon, and transfer it directly into the sugar syrup. After about 3 minutes, remove and transfer to a serving plate. Repeat with the remaining batter.

Sprinkle with some roasted pistachios.

How to Enjoy

• This is best served warm.

• The jalebi tastes great as is, but for a special occasion, pair it with plain dairy-free vanilla ice cream.

Special Pansache Dhonas

Steamed jackfruit cake

Jackfruit is showing up often on vegan menus these days. The unripe form of the fruit has become a popular meat alternative in different dishes because of its appearance and texture. Jackfruit has been used in various Asian cuisines for hundreds of years. India, Malaysia, Indonesia and the Philippines are some of the countries where jackfruit is grown and incorporated into the cuisine. In the southern part of India, a popular sweet preserve made of ripe jackfruit is commonly prepared, called chakka varati. When the fruit is in season (March through June), savory dishes like idichakka thoran are everyone's favorite stir-fry on the Kerala Sadhya menu on festive days, and on regular days as well. My favorite form of eating jackfruit are the chips and pappadām, both commonly consumed in Kerala. In Goan villages, jackfruits grow in abundance. This is a traditional Goan village–style cake, which is made typically when there is an excess of ripe jackfruit.

Yield: 6 to 8 servings * *Prep Time: 15 minutes* * *Cook Time: 1 hour*

1¼ cups (230 g) ripe (not young) jackfruit from a can (drained)

¾ cup (130 g) fine (not coarse) ravā aka sooji (semolina)

2 tsp (4 g) ground cardamom (elaichi)

½ cup (120 ml) full-fat coconut milk from a can (shaken)

1 cup (150 g) jaggery powder (see Tip)

12 to 15 unsalted, roasted cashews

Tip

Jaggery is a type of unrefined sugar that is made from sugar cane or palm. You can find a variety of jaggery sold in blocks or powder in most well-stocked South Asian grocery stores. The powdered variety works well in this recipe.

Puree the jackfruit in a blender without adding any water or syrup from the can. Set the jackfruit aside. Line a medium cake pan with parchment paper.

In a large skillet over medium heat, roast the ravā until it appears light brown, 10 to 12 minutes, stirring continuously, as the ravā can burn quickly. Transfer it to a large mixing bowl and set it aside to cool for 5 minutes. Stir in the ground cardamom and the coconut milk.

Add the jaggery powder to the bowl with the mixture. Break any big pieces of jaggery so that you get a smooth, lump-free batter. Add the pureed jackfruit to the bowl, and mix everything until well combined. Transfer the batter to the cake pan. Top the cake with cashews.

Prepare a steamer pot or Dutch oven. Add water, making sure the water level is below the top of the cake tin when placed inside the pot. Bring the water to a boil, reduce the heat to medium, and gently place the cake pan with the batter inside the pot or Dutch oven. Cover with the lid, and steam the cake until a toothpick inserted into the cake comes out clean, 30 to 35 minutes.

Remove the cake pan from the pot, and set it aside to cool for about 2 hours. Unmold the cake on to a plate, then cut it into slices, and serve at room temperature.

How to Enjoy

You can also toast the slices in a nonstick pan with a few spoonfuls of coconut oil until the surface turns slightly golden brown, and then serve them warm.

Thali

Thāli is a Hindi word that stands for a round platter. Thāli also means the dining format where a complete meal is served on a single plate, usually a metal one, typically comprised of smaller portions of multiple dishes—snacks (dishes like dhokla, bhajiyas), sabzis (gravies and/or stir-fries), dāl, rice, roti (flatbreads), salad, accompaniments (pāpad, pickles, chutneys) and sweet treats, served in matching little bowls. The key to a great thāli is balance of flavor and nutrition, and the dishes in a thāli incorporate ingredients that feature sweet, salty, astringent, pungent, sour and bitter flavors. You can celebrate colorful Indian food on a single platter, or on a banana leaf, like in many parts of south India, with these thāli meal ideas at your home, with a combination of various dishes from this cookbook. In India, you'll find thāli at several thāli-specific restaurants, and they are usually regional specific—Gujarati thāli, Rajasthani thāli, South Indian thāli, which are sometimes called "meals" in many parts of South India. Everything from its vibrant colors to the exhaustive variety of flavors, a thāli experience is a wholesome and fulfilling one. But the thāli I grew up eating in my home always had dishes from across India, and with the suggestions here, you, too, can create a simple plant-based one.

Layered Triangle Parātha + Lip-Smacking Gobi Bhuna +
Spongy Ravā Dhokla + Raita

Aromatic Parsi Berry Pulav + Mouthwatering Pānch Phoran Dāl +
Fresh Carrot Kosambari + Succulent Jalebi

Nourishing Kāla Chana Chāt + Colorful Vegetable Sabzi +
Flavorful Pāpad ki Sabzi + Basmati Rice

The thāli pictured to the left has
Mouthwatering Pānch Phoran Dāl + Scrumptious Dum Aloo Kashmiri +
Speedy Sev Tamātar + Silky Punjabi Kadhi with Pakoda + Smoky Baingan Bharta +
Raita + Simple Āte ka Halva + Refreshing Masālā Lemon Shikhanji

Recipes for Accompaniments and Other Essentials

Accompaniment	Directions
Date-Tamarind Chutney	To a large saucepan, add ½ cup (125 g) tamarind from a block and 20 pitted dates. Add hot, boiling water to the saucepan, just enough to cover the tamarind and dates. Bring the mixture to a boil, and turn off the heat. Using a sieve, strain the mixture into a bowl and discard the pulp. Add the strained mixture back into the saucepan, add about 30 ounces (1 kg) jaggery powder into the saucepan along with ½ tablespoon (5 g) Kashmiri red chili powder, 1 tablespoon (6 g) cumin powder, 1 tablespoon (18 g) kāla namak (black salt), ½ teaspoon ground ginger, salt to taste and 2½ cups (600 ml) water. Bring the mixture to a boil over medium-low heat for about 20 minutes. Cool completely, and store in an airtight container in the refrigerator for up to 2 days.
Mint-Cilantro Chutney	Thoroughly wash 1 cup (15 g) fresh cilantro and ½ cup (45 g) mint, and remove the tough stems, if any. Add the cilantro and mint to a blender along with 2 to 3 green chili peppers, 1 teaspoon fresh grated ginger, 1 teaspoon of chana dāl (dalia or roasted split chickpeas), ½ teaspoon kāla namak (black salt), salt to taste, 2 ice cubes and a few drops of water. Grind to a smooth paste. Store in an airtight container in the refrigerator for up to a day.
Garlic Chutney	Soak 12 whole dried Kashmiri red chilis in about 2 cups (480 ml) hot water for 15 minutes. To a blender, add the soaked chilis, 10 cloves of peeled garlic, 1 teaspoon ground cumin, 1 teaspoon of kāla namak (black salt), salt to taste and about ½ cup (120 ml) water. Grind to a fine paste. If it appears too thick, you may add some water. Store it in an airtight container in the refrigerator for up to 2 weeks. Make sure to use a clean, dry spoon each time you use the chutney, otherwise it will not last, even when refrigerated.
Cashew Cream	Soak 1 cup (140 g) raw, unsalted cashews in hot water for 20 minutes. Drain the cashews, and blend them with 1 cup (240 ml) of unsweetened, plain plant-based milk of choice until smooth and creamy. Store in an airtight container and use as needed in place of heavy cream. This can be stored in the refrigerator for up to a week.

Garam Masālā	In a skillet over medium heat, dry roast each separately—¼ cup (35 g) black peppercorns, ¼ cup (25 g) cloves, ¼ cup (20 g) coriander seeds, ¼ cup (24 g) cumin seeds, ¼ cup (20 g) cinnamon sticks, ¼ cup (25 g) fennel seeds, ¼ cup (25 g) black cardamom (badi elaichi) and 1 teaspoon crushed dried bay leaves (tej patta) until fragrant, about 3 minutes each, stirring continuously. Cool completely, and transfer them all together to a spice grinder and grind to a fine powder. Store in an airtight container.
Chāt Masālā	In a skillet over medium heat, dry roast 2 tablespoons (12 g) cumin seeds, 1 tablespoon (5 g) coriander seeds, ¼ teaspoon black peppercorns, 2 whole dried red chilies, 1 teaspoon of carom seeds, ½ teaspoon of cinnamon sticks and 2 whole cloves, and roast them together until fragrant, stirring continuously, about 4 minutes. Cool them completely, and transfer them to a spice grinder, add 2 tablespoons (16 g) dry mango powder, 1½ tablespoons (27 g) black salt, 1 tablespoon (18 g) salt, and 1 teaspoon ground ginger. Grind well, then transfer to an airtight container.
Raita	Mix together 1 cup (240 ml) whisked plain unsweetened dairy-free yogurt with ¼ cup (40 g) finely chopped onions, ¼ cup (45 g) diced tomatoes, ¼ cup (50 g) chopped cucumber, salt to taste, 1 teaspoon chāt masālā, ¼ teaspoon red chili powder and 1 teaspoon ground cumin. Add water as needed to thin it out, if needed.

Acknowledgments

Writing a cookbook is way harder than I had thought. From the time I decided on the idea for the book to this very moment when I am looking back on all that went into its creation, I realize how much my village came together to convert my dream to reality.

Shuba Iyer—thank you for being a collaborator from the very early days of the book. Your imaginative and colorful ceramic creations were the perfect vehicles to showcase the beauty and versatility of the Indian food in this book. Heartfelt thanks to you and your studio Kneaded Earth (www.kneadedearth.com).

Shekhar Bagawde—your creative genius was behind the YummyYatra logo, thank you!

Thank you to all my friends and family who tested the recipes and provided valuable feedback—Narayana Moorthy, Usha and Sanjay, Chirag and Archana, Kumaresh and Shuba, Preeti and Sameer, Geetha Krishnan, Ganesh and Brenda, Roopa Santosh, Sara Tercero (@betterfoodguru) and Sara (@thevegansara), Shyma Noordeen, Hetal Suratwala, Renuka Gusain, DeeDee Steele-Sigee, Adale, Balsara, Pooja Srivatsa, Evita Rodrigues, Nicole McLaren and Bianca Phillips.

Thanks to the expert team at Page Street Publishing who understood and gave expression to my vision for the book. Special thanks to Emily Archbold—you were the best editor I could have asked for. You were thorough, collaborative, understanding, flexible and a pleasure to work with.

Thank you to all my fellow bloggers and digital content creators who continue to inspire me with their creativity, knowledge and dedication to the craft.

The creation process was not easy, and there were times when I felt that my progress was slow. But every time I doubted myself, I had my people, my wonderful family and friends telling me that I was doing perfectly fine. My people are everything to me. I couldn't have written this book without their love, encouragement, and brilliant ideas.

To my loving parents, Narayana Moorthy and Usha Moorthy, thank you for always giving me the wings and freedom to fly. My passion for food comes from your incredible love for cooking and for the variety of soul-satisfying, and nutritious food you always made at home. Thank you for those cherished food memories that are ever so sweet.

Santosh, my multi-talented husband, your belief in me sometimes exceed my own. Thank you for supporting me every step of the way, including coming up with the very name "YummyYatra" that marries my three passions: food, travel and photography. Without you, I wouldn't have evolved to be this version of myself. Thank you for being my love and my number one critical editor.

Chirag, my amazing brother, sharing YummyYatra with the world would not have happened without your push. Thank you for all the behind-the-scenes work and for always being there for me.

My sweet sisters-in-law, Usha and Archana, thank you for your encouraging words and for patiently listening to me while I was discussing my ideas with you.

Gaia, my daughter, my raison d'être, you motivated me to stay true to my authentic voice throughout this book. Thanks to your inquisitiveness and love for cultures, you were a huge help in researching, testing, styling, writing, editing and photographing each and every recipe in this book. I love that you were my hand model for every picture, including the front and back covers of this book! You are the best!

Neo, my other baby, my beloved dog, thank you for being in my life. You are the inspiration for me being vegan. You being by my side through all those recipe-testing and manuscript-writing phases, with your calm, zen demeanor, made this process so much more easier.

And importantly, thank you to you, dear reader, for being the culmination of the journey of this book. I hope reading and cooking from this book gives you as much pleasure as I got from creating it for you.

About the Author

Anusha Moorthy Santosh is the creator of YummyYatra, where readers can discover delicious and flavorful vegan recipes. Anusha loves to cook and especially enjoys veganizing and reimagining classic recipes.

Her work has been featured in various vegan and vegetarian publications and she has collaborated with the world's leading vegan brands. Anusha has lived in multiple continents and has also traveled extensively across the globe; this has contributed to her wide culinary range. Her goal is to inspire everyone to eat clean and nutritious food.

Anusha currently lives in Alpharetta, Georgia, with her husband, Santosh; daughter, Gaia and their zen dog, Neo. Follow her on Instagram and TikTok @yummyyatra and enjoy her blog at yummyyatra.com.